Battlefields

Annual Review

Battlefields

Annual Review

Edited by

JON COOKSEY

Pen & Sword
MILITARY

First published in Great Britain in 2005 by
Pen & Sword Military an imprint of
Pen & Sword Books Ltd
47 Church Street
Barnsley
South Yorkshire
S70 2AS

Copyright © Jon Cooksey, 2005
Design and layout: Jon Wilkinson

ISBN: 1 84415 281 2

Printed and bound in Singapore by
Kyodo Printing Co (Singapore) Pte Ltd.

Pen & Sword Books Ltd incorporates the Imprints of
Pen & Sword Aviation, Pen & Sword Maritime, Pen
& Sword Military, Wharncliffe Local History, Pen and
Sword Select, Pen and Sword Military Classics and
Leo Cooper.

For a complete list of Pen & Sword titles please
contact
PEN & SWORD BOOKS LIMITED
47 Church Street, Barnsley, South Yorkshire, S70 2AS,
England
E-mail: enquiries@pen-and-sword.co.uk
Website: www.pen-and-sword.co.uk

CONTENTS

FRONT COVER IMAGE: TIM LYNCH
THIS PAGE MAIN IMAGE: TIM LYNCH

EDITOR'S INTRODUCTION

Battles, it has been said, are but a fleeting intrusion on the landscape. Even the most protracted of sieges - when set in the context of the vast sweep of recorded history - are but a blip on the radar. And whilst it is certainly true that it is the landscape and terrain that sculpts and shapes a battle, it is the combatants who have first to analyze that landscape and then grapple with its constraints and the forces of the elements in order to fight it - the more successful combatants often displaying more vision, seeing opportunities where others see none and sometimes even working 'outside the box' to outwit and overwhelm their adversaries. Win or lose, when any battle or siege takes place, physical evidence of the struggle is often left behind; a button torn off here, weapons and ammunition fragments there, perhaps burials of those killed in action, all of which, if not removed and taken elsewhere, eventually become obscured over time.

NOW, IN THE EARLY TWENTY FIRST CENTURY, as the interest in military history grows and what was once battlefield pilgrimage for the few becomes transformed into battlefield tourism for the many, the discipline of battlefield archaeology is assuming an increasingly influential role in providing an interpretation of the landscapes within which these violent events took place.

For four years from 2000 *Battlefields Review* magazine brought together some of the world's leading authorities on military history in order to bring battlefields to life for its readers. Last year saw the publication of the first *Battlefields Annual Review*, which carried on the best traditions of the magazine - this time in book form - by gathering together a superb cast of contributors, both professional and amateur military historians, who offered their own, unique perspectives on their chosen subjects. This year *Battlefields Annual Review* switches the spotlight onto battlefield archaeology - an essential element of the study of battles and battlefields - and again has assembled an impressive array of acknowledged specialists providing leading edge research in order to get below, and in some cases high above, the surface of their selected battlefields. Their contributions reveal how the people of the past - caught up in often horrific conflicts - lived just as much as how they died and what lessons the

people of the present can learn in order to preserve the world's battlefields for the education of future generations, in the broader context of present day imperatives for local, regional and national development.

There is news from Derek Batten on the 2004 season dig on the Little Bighorn battlefield and a round up, by Mike Dolamore, the present Chairman of the Durand Group, on the important work being done to explore, survey and disarm the subterranean tunnels beneath much visited sections of the WW1 battlefields of the Western Front. Staying with the theme of the Western Front, Andy Robertshaw and Alastair Fraser tell the remarkable story of the quest to find the location of a German dugout on the Somme in which the poet Wilfred Owen had sought shelter in early 1917. Although 'Owen's' dugout was never found, the resulting archaeological discoveries led to results no one in the team could have predicted.

Staying beneath the Western Front, this time below the surface of the Ypres Salient in Belgium, Franky Bostyn, Curator of the Memorial Museum Passchendaele 1917 and current Chairman of the Association for Battlefield Archaeology in Flanders, reports on the excavations, finds, history and restoration of a WW1 dressing station built by the Germans and captured by the British in 1917.

Professional archaeologist, author and Project Officer

for the Battlefields Trust, Glenn Foard and his colleague Tracey Partida update us on the progress of a database and resource assessment for Historic Scotland (HS). This work, on fields of conflict across Scotland, is intended to assist HS in determining how best to manage the important archaeological and historic landscape heritage. For his second contribution, Glenn turns his attention south of the border, to take us to the site of the first major battle of the Civil War in England at Edgehill and provides his perspective on the latest developments in, and possible consequences of, the ongoing archaeological survey of this key English battlefield.

From an important and well documented engagement of the English Civil War, Tim Lynch takes us to Tankersley Moor, an obscure northern battlefield of the same conflict and examines the issues surrounding the archaeology of sites of which relatively little is known or recorded.

Dr. Peter Haupt of the Johannes Gutenberg University of Mainz in Germany and Cain Hegarty, Sarah Newsome and Helen Winton of English Heritage provide a completely different perspective on battlefield archaeology in their contributions as they examine the role of remote sensing and aerial archaeology and their potential contribution to the study of military sites and landscapes. Taking to the air, Peter Haupt looks down on the region around Mainz in the Rhine Palatinate,

whilst Cain Hegarty, Sarah Newsome and Helen Winton fly over the Suffolk coast to reveal much about the military heritage of both regions, a heritage that is often invisible to those working on the ground.

Even further afield, Dr Adrian Mandzy of Morehead University, Kentucky, reports on new interpretations of the 1649 War between the Cossacks and the Polish-Lithuanian Commonwealth, supported by finds from archaeological excavations around the towns of Zboriv and Zbarazh in the Ukraine. Last but not least, Dan Sivilich's contribution - drawing on more than a decade of archaeological investigation - separates history from mythology to provide fresh insights into the fighting during the Battle of Monmouth, one of the largest battles of the American Revolutionary War.

There is much here about warfare and weaponry to read and reflect upon but, and most important of all, there is also much here about how the results of archaeological studies have continued to assist historians in piecing together the often personal details of those whose very lives were lost during the fighting and whose bodies, perhaps, were once thought to be lost for ever. As Martin Brown, co-organiser of the Annual National Army Museum Conference on Battlefield Archaeology once said, battlefield archaeology is about 'digging up people' and it is, after all, the people who matter.

ACKNOWLEDGMENTS

ONCE AGAIN, I OWE A GREAT DEBT OF THANKS to the contributors to *Battlefields Annual Review*. Last year I spoke of how contributors' passion, depth of knowledge and enthusiasm for their subject matter was infectious and this year has been no different. Their articles are, at once, erudite, illuminating and educating.

During the long process of editing and production – and there may be several twists and turns, much 'to-ing' and 'fro-ing', not to mention the occasional technological 'gremlin' along the way between raw text and images to the finished article - it has always been such a pleasure to be involved with the contributors in bringing their pieces to life on the page. At all times, and despite very busy schedules, they responded with a courtesy, professionalism and eye for detail for which I am truly grateful. That said any errors or omissions in the book are entirely due to me.

Jon Wilkinson has once more developed a series of design themes that are sensitive to the subject matter and he continues to look for new and innovative ways of enhancing the text. I thank him once again for his talent and his patience.

Although every attempt has been made to contact the copyright owners of illustrations or quotations included in the text, where this has not been possible I should be very happy to hear from those copyright holders affected.

Jon Cooksey

Reading 2005

Battlefields & History

For more than two decades Holts Battlefield and History Tours have been taking people to visit the battlefields where the men of Britain and the Commonwealth fought and died.

We have had the privilege, over the years, of visiting the battlefields of the First and Second World Wars, Vietnam and the Falklands in the company of those who served there. Now we more often take their children and grandchildren to visit these emotive places.

On each tour we have a brief wreath laying ceremony, in grateful remembrance of the sacrifices made.

Tours for 2006 include:

The Somme 90th Anniversary, Verdun, The Holocaust, Tunisia, Stalingrad, D-Day, Waterloo, Zulu War, Gettysburg, Scapa Flow, Agincourt.

To receive a copy of the current brochure please contact us on 01293 455356 or visit our website www.holts.co.uk

A00037-HT

BACK TO THE BEGINNING: LITTLE BIGHORN REVISITED - 2004

Almost everyone who has visited the Little Bighorn agrees that the autumn or 'Fall' season is a glorious time to visit the Custer Battlefield. It is over twenty years since the first archaeological survey was carried out in 1984, after a carelessly tossed cigarette caused the entire battlefield to be swept by fire the previous year. An archaeological survey was originally scheduled to take place in May 2004 but was put back until funds became available in the autumn. Although the 2004 survey would not come close to matching the 1984 dig in its size and scope, it nevertheless produced some dramatic results. Derek Batten reports.

By Derek Batten

IN PREVIOUS YEARS I HAVE BEEN VERY PRIVILEGED to be the only non-American involved with the archaeological work at the Little Bighorn Battlefield in Montana, USA. This began as long ago as 1984 and the work instigated by Doug Scott and Rich Fox was, both literally and figuratively, ground breaking in what has since developed as the academic discipline of Battlefield Archaeology.

As I was part of the team in 1985, 1989, and 1994, it was a thrill to be asked again to take part in a week's work in September 2004. A tarmac road links the Last Stand area, where Custer and his five troops of the Seventh Cavalry perished on the afternoon of 25th June

Archeological survey commences using metal detectors. BOB REECE

1876, with the Reno-Benteen defence site, some four and a half miles away. The rest of the regiment were able to hold out here for another three days until relieved on 28th June. This road is suffering, not only from the volume of traffic, but also from the size of those vast mobile homes that some American folk drive around in.

DETAILED SURVEY

I had not previously realised just how dangerous in places the route of the road is with no barriers at the sides. The photographs show this quite vividly. As a consequence, the US National Park Service decided to embark on a road-widening scheme involving some realignment but before the work commences, the opportunity was granted for a further detailed survey of the twenty metres of battlefield on each side of the road. The metal detecting carried out in 1984/85 never claimed to be 100% comprehensive and since then the detecting 'kit' has developed significantly as have detecting techniques. Even more advances have been made in surveying, so that with some of the latest Global Positioning Equipment, coordinate accuracy down to half a metre is now possible.

MAJOR FIND

Thus it was that on a Monday 13th September, some twenty hardy souls (Doug calls us the 'A team') gathered in the overcast and drizzly gloom of the early morning at the Reno - Benteen site and started working towards the Visitor's Center some way away. We

were soon in business, locating and digging the usual collection of junk: ring tabs, pieces of wire, fence staples and silver paper, etc., although within ten minutes or so our first battle related artefact was unearthed. And so it continued, the wet ground making walking tiring, until later that day we were suddenly rejuvenated with probably the major find of the week. One small area yielded eighteen .44/55 cartridge cases, almost certainly fired from one Trooper's Springfield carbine. It is known that a group of men had ventured out from the defensive perimeter to try and link up with Custer before being forced back by Indian attacks. At this very spot some brave individual gave rapid covering fire to his retiring colleagues.

THRILL

Over the next few days, the weather improved and by the end of the week it really was quite hot. Wednesday was an eventful day as we found ourselves working in Medicine Tail Coulee, the location for the depiction of the *Last Stand* in the movie, *Little Big Man*. We kept turning up metal hairgrips and eventually worked out that these had been used to secure the wigs worn by the many film extras portraying Sioux and Cheyenne.

A good number of spent cartridge cases were also found but the excitement was short lived as these were identified as the blanks used in the same film. But then a spent Remington .50/70 cartridge,

Unearthed, a .44 Henry bullet lays exactly where it fell, dropped by Custers men. BOB REECE

Bob Reece holds a Remington .50/70 round, a bullet which was issued to officers only. Could this have been fired by Custer? BOB REECE

albeit in pretty bad shape, was discovered. As Custer 'buffs' will testify the General was one of only a handful of officers who would have used ammunition of such a calibre. Had this been fired by the man himself? I guess there is no way of knowing, but the possibility was a thrill for us all.

TWO MOONS

Little Bighorn aficionados will know of the area of the battlefield known as Greasy Grass Ridge. The 1984 Dig identified this as a warrior position and a number of spent Henry repeating rifle cartridges were found then. But this Dig turned up .44 Sharps carbine cartridges. We know that Two Moons, a Northern Cheyenne chief who fought in the battle had such a weapon which is still in existence and to which Doug Scott has access. Firing pin imprints on the found cartridge cases will establish whether or not Two Moons was in action here.

During the week we also found three metal arrowheads. Twelve weeks of survey in previous years had revealed only nine such artefacts.

All told the five-day Dig produced some 340 battle related artefacts, mainly cartridge cases and bullets. Doug Scott will compare the data found in 2004 with that gathered from previous projects and he will perform ballistic tests, mapping and analysis which will no doubt reveal yet more facets of this intriguing and iconic conflict.

A Henry cartridge. Note the H imprinted on the head of the cartridge. BOB REECE

A metal arrow head found at the base of this soldier's marker. BOB REECE

PRELIMINARY ARTEFACT FINDS

We are just beginning the cleaning and detailed analysis of the materials so it will take some time to make final determinations. A few things will undoubtedly be reclassified as we get them cleaned and see more details but this list should give a good idea of what we found.

By Douglas Scott – Leading Archaeologist, Little Bighorn Battlefield

I DID CHECK THE NUMBERS AND TYPES of things found in earlier years in the same areas we walked for the road mitigation, and found that our original sampling design was very accurate in predicting the kinds of things we should and, indeed, did find. We estimated, based on some statistical sampling that the earlier work was about a 35% sample. That proved very accurate, but in some areas, like the Calhoun loop road, which we sampled heavily in 1994, we found 78% of the artefacts then (the total artefacts recovered includes all earlier work and that from the road work).

Preliminary sorting of the artefacts determined there are 337 individual or groups of artefacts recovered at 320 separate find spot locales. The table below is an initial sorting which determined that the following types of artefacts were recovered:

ARTEFACT	NUMBER FOUND
.45-55 cartridge cases	82
.45-55 unfired cartridges	6 *(one found 10 inches deep, probably indicating a rifle pit locale at Reno-Benteen)*
Benet primers (loose)	4
.45-caliber 405 grain bullets	47
.45-caliber 500 grain bullets	2 *(post-battle)*
.50-70 cartridge cases	10
.45-caliber cases fired in .50 guns	5
.50-caliber 450 grain bullets	12
.44-caliber cases fired in Henrys	41
.44-caliber cases fired in other guns	2
.44-caliber 220 grain bullets	15
.44 Colt unfired	1
.44 or .45-caliber Sharps bullet	1
.44 Evans case?	1
.44 Short cases?	2
.44-77 Sharps cases	2
.44-40 cases	5
.45 Colt cases	3
.45 Colt cartridges unfired	2 *(one failed to detonate)*
.45 Colt bullets	2
.56-50 Spencer cases	2
.56-50 Spencer cases other	3 *(block or circular firing pin imprints)*
.50 Spencer bullets	2

ARTEFACT	NUMBER FOUND
.36 spherical balls	2
.44 or .45 spherical balls	3
.50 spherical balls	5
Unidentified lead fragments	3
Other bullets (Modern)	7
Iron arrowheads	3
Gun parts	3 *(barrel band, Colt backstrap screw, and a possible band fragment)*
Canteen Stoppers	2
Trouser buttons	4
Boot nails	2 *(one loose, one group with leather fragment)*
Horseshoes	4
Horseshoe nails	2
Horse bone	1 *(intermediate carpus right front leg)*
Lithic debris (prehistoric)	1
Flake Miscellaneous	27 *(including some modern items, as well as boot heel plate, suspender grip, knife handle, possible boiler handle, ferrel from a Civil War era cleaning brush, and an 1876 cartridge belt buckle post-battle).*

SCOTTISH BATTLEFIELDS – DATABASE AND RESOURCE ASSESSMENT

During winter 2004-5 the Battlefields Trust has been preparing a database and resource assessment for Historic Scotland on fields of conflict across the whole country. The work is intended to assist them in determining how best to manage this important archaeological and historic landscape resource. Having decided not to follow the useful but highly selective approach taken by England, where a Register of Historic Battlefields was established in 1995, Historic Scotland are seeking the information that will enable more appropriate strategies to be defined for all sites. The data from the project should of course also prove of use for other research purposes and be of more general interest.

By Glenn Foard & Tracey Partida

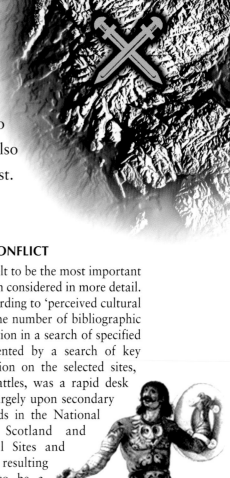

First of all we have enhanced the Scottish content of the Battlefield Trust's UK Fields of Conflict database, which the Trust is developing to provide basic information on battlefields and other fields of conflict of the pre-industrial period in England, Northern Ireland, Scotland and Wales. The enhanced database does not claim to represent comprehensive coverage of all sites, although an attempt has been made to ensure that all located battles as well as iconic lesser actions are included. Sieges, that is military action consisting primarily of assaults upon heavily fortified sites, are excluded from the current study, as are naval actions because both represent a distinctly different resource which requires separate assessment. A classification of types of action has been applied, distinguishing battles from other lesser actions, including skirmishes, clan warfare and other events of civil unrest. For each action a bibliography of secondary sources has been compiled from a specified list of battlefield and related publications. An initial assessment of value has been made for every database entry.

IMPORTANT FIELDS OF CONFLICT

A selection of what were felt to be the most important fields of conflict has then been considered in more detail. This selection was made according to 'perceived cultural significance', as defined by the number of bibliographic entries recovered for each action in a search of specified secondary works, complemented by a search of key online indexes. Data collection on the selected sites, almost all of which were battles, was a rapid desk based study exercise based largely upon secondary published sources, on records in the National Monuments Record for Scotland and information from the local Sites and Monuments Records. The resulting gazetteer does not claim to be a comprehensive statement as to the current state of knowledge of each of the selected sites, though where possible the most recent publications on the battle and battlefield have been consulted. Finally the possible extent of action was viewed against both modern OS mapping and geological mapping to assess the current state of development

and likely overall archaeological and interpretive potential of the sites.

There are now 358 Scottish entries on the database, representing 343 separate actions, with 15 'alternate' sites for battlefields, such as Bannockburn (Stirling, 1314), where there is uncertainty as to location. Of this total, 39 are classified as battles and a further 19, from the medieval period, are identified as probably justifying classification as battles. A further 100 lesser actions have been verified as genuine engagements. This class of action is almost certainly grossly under represented as many are only likely to be identified by an extensive search of specialist historical work on individual war periods, a task which could not be undertaken within the current project. Also on the database there are 3 massacres (of which the best known is Glencoe, 1692), 1 judicial combat (North Inch or Battle of the Clans, 1396) and 2 sites which are sometimes included in lists of battles but where even though armies faced each other no action took place (Carberry Hill, 1657 and Hill of Rowan, 1307). The remaining 185 actions, of which 83 are wholly undated, are as yet unverified. Many of these were minor clan conflicts identified solely through local traditions, a significant proportion of which appear to be spurious.

POTENTIAL

The main focus of attention has been on the battles, where there is generally the greatest potential for the field of conflict to yield significant information about the action and about warfare in general. With specific exceptions, there is a general fall off in the number of battles as one moves back in time. To a degree this may be influenced by a decrease in quantity and quality of primary documentation for earlier centuries, which certainly becomes a major problem by the early medieval period. But it also reflects the generally accepted view that, particularly in the medieval period, battle was very much a matter of last resort, as opposed to sieges and lesser actions. There are also significantly fewer battles in the 18th century together with very few lesser actions, all of which can be broadly classified and located. For earlier centuries there are not only more

Map legend:
- ⬤ Battles
- ★ Possible battle sites
- ⬤ Lesser actions
- ○ Unverified sites

(Map locations labelled: Inverness, Dundee, Stirling, Glasgow, Edinburgh)

'There are now 358 Scottish entries on the database, representing 343 separate actions, with 15 'alternate' sites for battlefields...'

battles but also substantially more skirmishes, as well as a large number of unverified and possibly largely spurious minor actions. The high number for the 17th century is influenced by the intense action in the civil war and the early phases of the Jacobite risings. The 16th century in contrast sees a significant fall in numbers.

TRANSITION

For comparative purposes the number of battles in England can be compared in graph form alongside those from Scotland. This shows that the trends in the Scottish sample are broadly mirrored in England, though the number in England is generally higher. The exceptions

SCOTTISH FIELDS OF CONFLICT

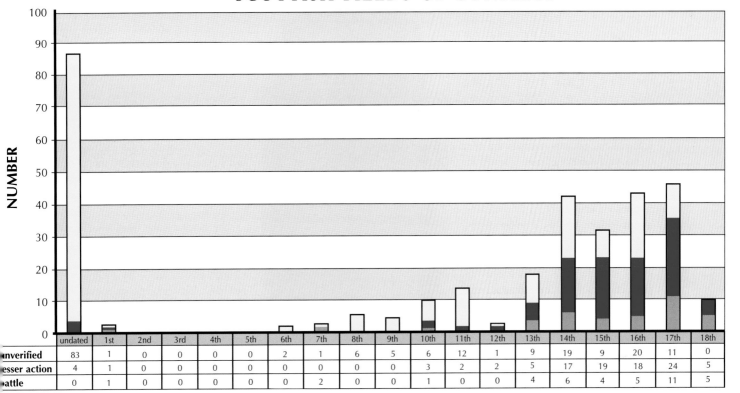

	undated	1st	2nd	3rd	4th	5th	6th	7th	8th	9th	10th	11th	12th	13th	14th	15th	16th	17th	18th
unverified	83	1	0	0	0	0	2	1	6	5	6	12	1	9	19	9	20	11	0
lesser action	4	1	0	0	0	0	0	0	0	0	3	2	2	5	17	19	18	24	5
battle	0	1	0	0	0	0	0	2	0	0	1	0	0	4	6	4	5	11	5

SCOTTISH FIELDS OF CONFLICT BY CENTURY   **CENTURY**

SCOTTISH & ENGLISH BATTLES COMPARED

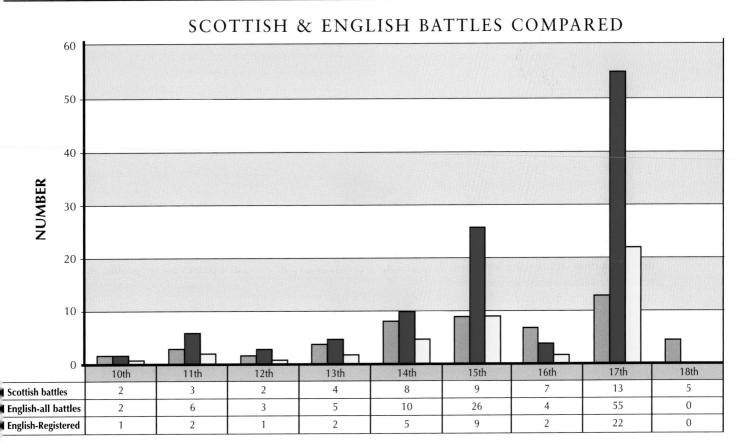

	10th	11th	12th	13th	14th	15th	16th	17th	18th
Scottish battles	2	3	2	4	8	9	7	13	5
English-all battles	2	6	3	5	10	26	4	55	0
English-Registered	1	2	1	2	5	9	2	22	0

SCOTTISH AND ENGLISH BATTLES BY CENTURY   **CENTURY**

are significant. The massive increase in England compared to Scotland in the 15th and 17th centuries are a result of the number of actions in the Wars of the Roses and the intensity of action in England during the Civil Wars. In both these periods not only the number but also the scale of the actions tends to be of a quite different order of scale in Scotland compared to England, with for example a battle like Alford (Aberdeenshire, 1645) involving about 5000 troops compared to Marston Moor (Yorkshire, 1644) with well over 40,000. By contrast it is in Scotland that the number of 16th century battles is greatest and, as this is a critical period in the transition of warfare from that dominated by the archer to that dominated by musket and pike, these Scottish battlefields, and most notably Pinkie (East Lothian, 1547), are a particularly important resource. It is also only in Scotland that there were full-scale battles that took place during the 18th century, again making these sites an important research resource.

The Aberlemno stone depicting scenes from the Battle of Nechtanesmere.

ERIC WALKER

LOCATION

One significant limitation in the database for Scotland can be seen by comparison with actions prior to the 10th century in England, but the vast majority of the pre 10th century actions have never been securely located to any site. A systematic search to add these early medieval actions should ideally be undertaken, but this task has a low priority given our inability at present to recognise the actions archaeologically. Thus there is a limited likelihood that any more of these sites can be located, with even the potentially most securely located of early battles, Nechtansmere (Angus, 685), still posing substantial problems.

The Battlefields Trust would like to acknowledge the assistance of various staff in Historic Scotland, the Royal Commission on the Ancient and Historic Monuments of Scotland, also staff in most of the local authority Sites and Monuments Records across Scotland and various other specialists who have advised on the work. A digital copy of the report, gazetteer and database is to be deposited with the National Monuments Record and each Sites and Monuments Record and it is intended that they can be made accessible online later during 2005. It is hoped that during 2005-7, as part of a proposed wider enhancement by the Battlefields Trust, the results of the project can be included on the Trust's UK Battlefields Resource Centre, an Internet resource on battlefields which currently deals only with English battlefields:

http://www.battlefieldstrust.com/resource-centre

The plain memorial cairn which stands near the site of the former Mere where Brudei and his Pictish army trapped Egfrith. ERIC WALKER

SUBTERRANEAN BATTLEFIELD ARCHAEOLOGY ON THE WESTERN FRONT - A DURAND GROUP UPDATE

Thousands of visitors, travelling either independently or in organised parties, now visit the battlefields of the British sector of the Western Front of WW1. In many cases they walk across tranquil fields and are inevitably drawn to the surface features that are the great memorials to the dead or grim reminders of battles fought almost a century ago - some of which, like the Lochnagar mine crater on the Somme - are very significant indeed. What they do not see is what lies beneath their feet - the thousands of metres of tunnels dug by those who waged a war deep underground. The tunnel systems are still there, as are remnants of the explosives used in this subterranean battlefield. The exploration of these systems and the subsequent reporting of their condition and of finds of any unexploded material, has almost become the sole province of the Durand group, so much so that it now advises official institutions on the condition of the tunnel systems beneath the ground for which they bear responsibility. It is slow, dirty and dangerous work but ultimately those visitors to some of the key sites of the war on the Western Front have good cause to thank the group for the hazardous work it undertakes. Durand Group Chairman, Mike Dolamore, gives an update on the work of the group so far.

By Lieutenant Colonel (Retd) Mike Dolamore MBE - Deputy Chairman, The Durand Group

THE DURAND GROUP WAS FORMED IN 1998 as the exploratory vehicle for a small group of like-minded enthusiasts with a passion for 'military related subterranean features', especially those relating to the First World War. Readers of *Battlefields Review* magazine may recall some of the organisation's early work beneath the Vimy and Beaumont Hamel battlefields, as detailed in the irregular 'News from the Durand Group' articles. Seven years on and I am pleased to say that, despite an early tragedy - the death of our colleague, Lieutenant Colonel Mike Watkins - the group has prospered, attained charitable status, and has gained something of an international reputation for its expertise in WWI tunnelling and mining activities. This article is intended to bring the reader up to date with some of the projects undertaken by The Durand Group since it last graced the pages of *Battlefields Review* and draws on work already published in *The RLC Review* and the *Journal of The Institute of Explosive Engineers*.

A BRIEF HISTORY

The first recorded incident of mine warfare in WW1 took place along the Givenchy-Festubert front, close to the Franco-Belgian border, on 20th December 1915. At 10.25hrs in the morning a huge series of explosions destroyed 1000 yards of the front line and its occupants - Indian troops of the Sirhind Brigade. Those who were not killed broke and fled leaving a gaping hole in the line that was only closed after fierce fighting. First honours in the underground war had gone to the Germans. The British response was swift with offensive counter-operations commenced by Brigade Mining Sections within days. However, in late 1914 the British Army was neither equipped nor trained for this type of work and it was clear that a more coordinated response was required.

The man who provided the impetus and coordination was Major John Norton Griffiths; the MP for Wednesbury and the head of a large

Right: The Tunnel-Master, Major John Norton Griffiths.

firm of engineering contractors with extensive mining experience from around the world. Within weeks he had convinced the War Office of the need for specialist mining companies and by the end February 1915 170 Tunnelling Company RE had been formed and was mining in Flanders. Mining activity increased tremendously throughout 1915 and early 1916 with a peak being reached in June of that year when, along the line of the British front, a combined total of 227 mines were fired by British and German forces; one mine every three hours.

The British mining effort grew to encompass 3 Canadian, 3 Australian, 1 New Zealand and 25 Imperial Tunnelling Companies and the Australian Electrical and Mechanical Mining and Boring Company - colloquially known as the 'Alphabetical Company'. Commanded by a Major with 17 other officers in support a typical Tunnelling Company strength was around 550 ranks with up to 600 infantry in direct support of each Company's mining effort. Between July 1916 and June 1917 there were some 30-40,000 British troops involved in mining activity alone and amongst all the belligerents the total approached 120,000 men.

Along the 80 mile length of the Western Front entrusted to the British and other Imperial forces certain areas became mining 'hotspots'. From north to south significant mining activity took place around Hooge, near Ypres and along the length of the Messines Ridge, at Aubers Ridge and around Festubert, at Loos, to the north of and around Arras, and along the Somme front at Beaumont Hamel, Gommecourt and at La Boiselle. Vimy Ridge in particular became very active and during 1916 became the most heavily mined place on earth. The opus magnus of mining operations took place along the Messines-Wytschaete Ridge to the south of Ypres in 1917. At 03.10hrs on 7th June 1917 nineteen mines, totalling just less than 1 million lbs of explosive, tore the ridge apart, killing as many as 10,000 Germans in the process.

WINNING THE UNDERGROUND WAR

At first the British and French tunnellers were very much on the defensive and this dictated where and how they mined. Single drive galleries tended to be the norm as the allied tunnellers sought to counter the German miners. However, as the allies and especially the British tunnellers got to grips with their enemy counterparts the scope and scale of their mining operations increased and more complex systems were constructed. Multi-galleried offensive systems were driven forward and deeper level defensive systems constructed.

As mining increased in intensity so the nature of the ground war began to be influenced by it as the terrain over which operations were conducted was altered. Huge craters began to appear amongst the myriad of shell holes transforming the surface into the moonscape so evocative of the Great War. By mid-1916, at the height of mining operations, the British in particular seized the initiative from the Germans and from this point on until the spring offensive in 1918, when a war of movement was once again possible, the Germans were very much on the back foot.

MINING PRINCIPLES

The design of a mine system would largely depend upon the geography of the terrain, the tactical considerations of the troops above and what and how the opposing miners were doing in the same area. The British front was broken down into sectors, each the responsibility of one or more Tunnelling Companies. At Vimy Ridge a number of stand-alone offensive mines were driven at a depth of 30-60 foot all along the front. Underpinning the offensive mines was a series of deeper level defensive systems; the primary purpose of these being not for fighting an offensive underground war but to protect the British lines from the German miners by listening for, intercepting and destroying their workings. 'O' Sector, which will be discussed later, is an example of such a deep defensive system.

A generic defensive mine system would typically comprise a main lateral gallery running parallel to, and just in front of, the British front line. Typically the main lateral could be up to 1000 metres in length and would be around 25 metres (60-80 feet) underground although German systems as deep as 50 metres (150 feet) are recorded on the Somme. Leading off from the main lateral, and running out under No Man's land, would be

A British officer with stethoscope listening for German mining under the Somme battlefield.

Graffiti left by British tunnellers and attached infantry men whilst spending endless hours listening for German mining activity.

a series of fighting tunnels at the end of which would be established listening posts. It was in these posts, deep underground, that the attached infantrymen and the tunnellers themselves would spend many hours listening for signs of German mining activity. Unsurprisingly, it is in the listening posts that Durand Group members frequently find extensive graffiti. In large systems, such as the deep defensive systems at Vimy Ridge, there could be upwards of 20-25 fighting tunnels/listening posts in use at any one time. With some notable exceptions (Verdun in particular) the French tunnellers tended to use single drive tunnels rather than extensive systems like the British. The Germans also tended not to dig main laterals with a myriad of fighting tunnels and listening posts but to group together 3 or 4 galleries accessed by a single shaft head.

Access to the main lateral was via galleries leading to the surface. The entrance points to these galleries could be in the main firing line, in the support lines or off communication trenches or other features depending upon the terrain and the tactical situation. In some early mine galleries the entrance points were actually in shell holes out in No Man's land. These galleries could be a few tens of metres long or, as in the case of the Kruisstaat mine up at Messines, some 2,160 feet long - over 650 metres. The number of access points would also vary depending upon the size of the mining system. It was preferable to have a minimum of two access points for obvious safety reasons. However, simple offensive drives often only had one entrance whilst the deep defensive systems, such as 'O' Sector, had nine in total.

These access tunnels either took the form of vertical shafts down to a tunnel connecting with the main lateral or an inclined gallery. In the chalk lands of the Artois and Somme regions the British tended to prefer inclined galleries whilst in the clay of Flanders shafts tended to be easier to sink and maintain. The French tunnellers generally seemed to prefer inclined galleries whilst the German almost invariably used shafted entrances after late 1915. British inclined galleries were typically 4 feet 6 inches wide by 5 feet high and with a 45∞ slope. Records of German mine workings investigated by French tunnellers at Bois Sabot in October 1915 indicate both shaft entrances and very steep 70∞ inclined galleries measuring 4 feet by 2 feet 7 inches.

There were a number of different explosive effects that could be achieved and which consequently categorise the mines that were fired. The common offensive mine was designed to destroy trench lines, defensive features and kill the enemy. The explosive charge would tend to be very large in order to cause the requisite effect. Typically offensive mines would consist of several tens of thousands of pounds of explosive. In the attack on the Messines Ridge the mines were typically around the 40-50,000 lb mark with the largest mine fired during the war being the St Eloi charge consisting of an astonishing 95,600 lbs of ammonal. Obviously the ground, the depth of the charge and the size and type of explosive used all determined the surface effect and the size and shape of the resultant crater. Huge craters could be formed by these offensive mines. It was not untypical for the craters to reach 150-200 feet across and 50-60 feet deep.

A variant of the normal offensive mine was the Fougasse mine. This described a mine charge intended for purely surface effects. For example it was common for Fougasse mines to be fired in the middle of No Man's land where the aim was to create high lips around the crater which could then be seized and consolidated by the infantry thus advancing the line. Alternatively Fougasse mines could be used to form blocks in the crater fields as with the Durand mine. They could also be used to screen parts of the battlefield from enemy machine gun posts and other weapon systems. An overcharged fougasse mine could also deliberately cause tons of debris to be hurled over defensive strongpoints and other features. In the 'E' Sap workings at La Bassèe Canal in the spring of 1916, 254 Tunnelling Company had used just such a Fougasse mine to form a defendable lip on the British side of an existing mine crater whilst denying the Germans the same and destroying both surface features and sub-surface mine workings.

THE P73G3 CAMOUFLET MINE

In the counter-mining battle the normal type of mine fired was the camouflet. Typically consisting of only a few hundred pounds of explosive, the aim of a camouflet mine was to destroy enemy workings without causing a surface crater. Although The Durand Group had previously extensively explored the La Folie tunnel system during 1998 the explorations had not been exhaustive and an outstanding project involved the technical investigation, and render safe if necessary, of a small camouflet mine charge in a forward listening post off the P73G3 fighting tunnel in the south of the system. The presence of a camouflet mine had been suspected for some time as the remains of a hastily laid firing cable had been found in the approach tunnel leading up to the chamber and the remnants of chalk tamping was still visible. It had been noted also that the firing cable appeared to be a pair of simple electrical wires rather than the more normal armoured cables. Furthermore the listening post that one would expect to step down into from the approach tunnel was now level with the tunnel flooring suggesting that something had been buried in the chamber. Of greater interest and relevance however was the discovery of an improvised listening device on the lip of the chamber. Formed from a beaten-out biscuit tin the conical listening device was still connected to the remains of air hosing that led back some considerable way to what appeared to have been a sentry post on the main lateral as some clips of .303 ammunition were found at this point.

From surviving mining plans of the La Folie system it was clear that the listening post itself was extremely near an approaching German tunnel. Evidence supporting this was also found in the weekly mine reports of 172 Tunnelling Company around the end of November 1916. In the report for the week ending 30 November 1916 the British tunnellers record *'enemy working continuously in front of P73G3. Talking is very distinct, also filling bags etc. Distance about 30 feet'*. Two weeks later the report of 14 December records that *'Enemy listener enters gallery about 25 feet from P73G3'*. On January 6th 1917 the British blew a camouflet in the chamber of P73G3 which just broke through to the surface as *'the enemy had been heard very close'*. Although there are no further references to the existing G3 tunnel it is typical in location of having been thrown out around the broken ground of the 6th January camouflet suggesting that further German activity had been heard and this new camouflet was set to catch them. If this was the case then the distance from the mine chamber to the German workings may have been as little as 10 feet or less.

All of the evidence suggested if this was a camouflet mine then it had been hastily laid and a simple listening device fashioned to listen for when the Germans broke into the British chamber. It was assumed that the mine would then have been fired with the intention of killing the German miners as well as collapsing their tunnel system. The existence of the improvised listening device was particularly interesting as it bore all the hallmarks of a well-known and documented officer of 172 Tunnelling Company - Second Lieutenant Brisco who was subsequently killed on 9 April 1917 exploring German mine shafts following the successful Canadian capture of the ridge. Prior to coming to Vimy Ridge 172 Company had been working at the notorious Bluff, further north along the line at the Ypres-Commines canal. There in November 1915 the Company had broken back into one of their old galleries only to find that the Germans had got there first. Consequently, one Second Lieutenant Brisco had placed a small charge within feet of the German listening post and;

> *'...also an improvised listening apparatus consisting of a funnel, made from an army biscuit tin, inserted into a length of rubber piping. The piping was carried through the charge and the ten feet of tamping back along [the] gallery, and for some time every movement and conversation of the Germans at this point could be heard distinctly'.*

In all likelihood it is probable that the camouflet mine the Group had found was also the work of the illustrious Brisco.

As well as satisfying both historical and technical curiosities about the P73G3 camouflet mine there remained the more pressing need to confirm whether it posed a safety threat. The existence of the charged and primed Durand Mine the year before had confirmed the fears that although the La Folie system, unlike all others, had been continuously accessible since WW1 live mine charges still remained in situ. From a public safety viewpoint it was therefore necessary to confirm to the

The improvised listening apparatus used to listen in on enemy movement and left by Brisco ninety years ago.

Canadian authorities whether the P73G3 chamber posed any threat. Although not designed to break surface the January 6th 1917 camouflet that had broken surface had indicated that it was a possibility, although a remote one. The render safe operation was undertaken by the qualified UK Ammunition Technical Officers of the Group.

Like the Durand Mine the P73G3 chamber was readily accessible, in that there was no need for any access excavations or tamping removal. However, the approach tunnel was not large and at a typical dogleg just before the chamber reduced in size to a mere 2'6" high by 3' wide. Indeed the chamber itself was no more than 4-5 feet across and high. Manoeuvring was therefore fairly difficult and any work on what was buried beneath the chalk debris surface of the chamber could only be undertaken from the lip of the chamber. Coupled with a low oxygen level within the chamber and clouds of chalk dust thrown up from the slightest of movements the render safe procedure proved awkward and hazardous.

Once the first few inches of chalk debris had been removed from the floor of the chamber the first of the familiar orange rubber-coated charge bags became visible. These appeared to be in good condition with the wooden sealing battens still in place but with the securing bolts rusted solid. After cutting into the first of these the familiar grey/silver colour of ammonal explosive was observed. Having determined that a mine charge was indeed present it was next necessary to find the primer bag. This bag was found to lay towards the top of the stack rather than in the middle, as was anticipated. Clearly the main stack had been in place for some time prior to the camouflet mine being finally set. Once it became clear that the Germans were on the verge of breaking into the chamber an improvised primer bag had been constructed and placed on top of the stack before being covered with a few spare charge bags and the tamping hurriedly put in place. The primer bag was found to contain two 2oz waxed dry guncotton primers with badly corroded, and highly sensitive, Detonators Electric No 13 Mk III inserted tightly into the primers. These were very carefully removed and packaged and subsequently transported out of the tunnel system for disposal by the French demineurs. Further investigation of the stack revealed no additional ignition systems and the final size of the mine was estimated to be around 600lbs or so.

'O' SECTOR CONQUERED

The Durand Group originally attempted to gain access to the 'O' sector deep defensive tunnel system in the southern part of the Vimy site in 1997/98. Tragically, a trench collapse in June 1998 during preliminary investigative work, killed founding member and leading light of the group Lieutenant Colonel Mike Watkins. Following this tragedy 'O' Sector was put on hold for a couple of years and it was not until 2000 that the Group returned to tackle the system. By this time the weather had begun to open up the trench line stairway leading into the O.64.E incline tunnel winch chamber; one of only three of the original nine inclines into the system located within the boundaries of the Canadian site. Ironically this stairway had already started to subside in late 1997 and some initial excavation work was undertaken. However, the extent of the infill was such that these preliminary efforts had been abandoned in favour of investigating the other accessible approach tunnels, all of which turned out to be inaccessible.

By mid 2000, the infill of the O.64.E stairway had subsided to such an extent that the entrance into the winch chamber itself was visible and appeared to suggest that the chamber was only partially filled. This also raised hopes that the incline tunnel down onto the main lateral may only be partially filled thus giving us access into the system. Excavating the O.64.E winch chamber stairway therefore now appeared to be the simplest of all the access options open to the Group. However, before committing to an extensive clearance operation it was agreed that it would be necessary to get a better appreciation of the extent of the infill in the incline tunnel. To do this remote endoscopic equipment was used. This equipment enabled us to put a camera down into the winch chamber which showed that it was indeed only partially filled and suggested that the incline tunnel itself may be accessible. Having determined that the O.64.E incline tunnel was a practical engineering option plans were drawn up for the excavation of the winch chamber stairway in September 2000.

The actual excavation down to the winch chamber proved a fairly straightforward affair with the line of the original stairway being picked up early on and some of the original wooden risers and flats being found in situ although in an advanced state of decay. Half way down the stairway the excavation was widened up beyond the original line so that a safety cage could be constructed to support the walls of the trench. Massive wooden pillars with cross-frames supported by acro-props were used to provide a secure working environment in which the lower level of the stairway could be accessed. During this work we recovered several hundred rounds of SAA as well as a wide range of other artefacts representing trench life in WW1. Of particular note, however, were the recoveries of a British hobnail boot, complete with the remains of a foot, and a complete trench brazier in excellent condition. The latter is currently undergoing restoration work with the Arras municipal archaeology department.

Once the winch chamber was within reach work stopped whilst an air hose was inserted into the winch chamber. This was necessary to provide a safe working environment within the chamber. One of the major secondary dangers facing the original miners was gas poisoning, particularly carbon monoxide (CO), arising from the subterranean explosions and many records exist of incidents in which tunnellers were lost to this hazard. Indeed, one of the best documented gas poisoning incidents occurred in 'O' sector on 21 August 1916 when nine soldiers lost their lives following the explosion of a German mine close to O.65.D. The retention of CO within fissures in chalk was a well-documented hazard at the time and the Group's own experiences in the La Folie sector have indicated that it remains so today.

Having cleared down the stairway into the chamber it was with some disappointment that the Group found that, contrary to the indication of the remote endoscopic examination, the incline was blocked solid approximately 30 feet down the slope. What was unclear was whether this was merely a localised blockage or solid infill all the way down to the 80 foot deep tunnel leading to the main lateral. If the former case this posed significant safety problems for further work as the cap of chalk debris could be merely a few feet thick and overlying a 45 degree, 8 foot by 8 foot void at least 50 feet in depth. If the latter then there was the unpalatable prospect of having to shift in excess of 40 tons of chalk debris in order to gain access.

The Group returned to 'O' sector in June 2001 with the aim of clearing the winch chamber itself of debris and exploring the nature of the blockage in the incline. The discovery of several No.5 Mk I hand grenades in the

Looking from the inside of the winch chamber at the shored entrance.

top layers of debris on the floor forced the Group to manually clear the winch chamber rather than use any mechanical means. Three days of work and 5 tons of debris later the floor had been dropped some 10 feet although the original level had yet to be reached, suggesting that the original height of the chamber had been at least 20 feet. During this process the stumps of the original six wooden pillars upon which the double-differential winch pulley apparatus had been located were discovered. However, there was no sight of the winch platform itself and it became increasingly clear that this had collapsed some considerable time before and, in all likelihood, slid down the incline where it could have been part of the reason for the blockage. Nevertheless, the Group did recover the winch itself, complete with winch cable and handles.

By careful probing it was determined that in all probability the blockage was solid and so in September 2001 we returned with commercial miniveyors, provided by Reko Products Ltd who had kindly agreed to sponsor the Group. The use of this equipment greatly speeded up the clearance of debris and as the Group moved down the incline the imprints of where the wooden rail sleepers had originally been became visible although the sleepers themselves had long since decayed away. In the course of a further week's work the Group were able to clear the whole of the infill down to the level of the main lateral although the actual breakthrough came at the very last minute of work on the last day and members had to endure another frustrating 3 month wait before the team could be brought back together to complete the clearance and so begin the exploration.

Before the system could be explored however, the Group cleared the base of the incline in order to be able to freely move our emergency casevac stretcher should it be required. In doing this yet another excellent find was

British hobnail boot.

A Hand Grenade No.5 Mk I.

Brazier still in a trench.

Bogey wheels from the winches.

*Ammanol bags found in
disarray in explosive store.*

made as the rubber wheels of one of the two original winch trolley bogeys emerged from the rubble, soon to be joined by its sister bogey. With the exception of the decayed woodwork this meant that all of the various metallic components of the winch system had been retrieved and would be able to be preserved and the equipment reconstructed for display purposes.

The initial exploration of 'O' sector in December 2001 revealed that the northern half of the system was very much as the various plans had suggested with one or two notable exceptions. Half way along the main lateral the Group first discovered an un-mapped 30 feet deep shaft. Whether this was an underground well, water sump or shaft to a lower level remains unclear. Certainly the shaft is water filled on some occasions and although there are indications of a tunnel just beginning to be driven out from its bottom, it goes nowhere and evidence for one or other option remains inconclusive. Further along up the O.63.E incline tunnel the Group also discovered an explosives store with a disorganised array of ammonal-filled mine charge bags and sandbags. Amongst the several hundred pounds of viable explosive littering the chamber the Group also recovered a small British mobile charge. This caused great excitement as although the existence of these charges is witnessed in contemporary books and their use witnessed in War Diaries, very few have survived. These charges were used by attacking troops to blow up German dugouts and mine entrances.

After 4 years hard work and one death it appeared that 'O' sector had finally given up its secrets and yet, the system was to have one last laugh on the Group. Half way down the system where the main lateral runs under the A26 autoroute, Group members turned a dogleg to find themselves confronted by a breezeblock wall blocking their way. It appeared that in the course of their work to construct the A26 the builders had broken into the O.63.D higher level offensive mine tunnel that the

Group discovered inter-connected with the lower level defensive system. They had clearly undertaken a preliminary investigation of the system and decided to block and infill that section under the path of the autoroute with concrete but had then failed to record this information anywhere!

The inability to go further was disappointing as the most interesting aspects of 'O' sector lay in the now inaccessible southern half, including the tempting prospect of access into the Lichfield Subway and the German mining system. Nevertheless the amount of survey and recording work still to be undertaken on the northern half of the system is immense despite early publication of the Group's preliminary findings. Tantalisingly, after some additional research it now appears likely that there is another abandoned camouflet mine in the higher level O.65.C.2 offensive mine tunnel close to Chassery crater.

GERMAN TROOPS IN THE B9 CRATER

Having been so close to the German workings during the render safe of the P73G3 camouflet mine attention has also been given to finding a way into them. To the Group's knowledge no access has yet been gained by anyone into German mine workings. Unlike the British workings the documentary record for the German operations is far less complete. In the Vimy area the Group has had to rely on preliminary map sketches made by Brisco and others of the German workings following their capture on 9th April 1917 and the British observations. According to this evidence access into the German workings that were being progressed towards P73G3 was from the nearby B9 crater; which was still completely overgrown.

In May 2004 a project was undertaken to attempt to find the entrance to the German workings. The 172 Tunnelling Company plans of the German system suggested that the entrance to Tunnel No.21 was in the west side of the crater where there were some noticeable slumps in the ground surface. A British reconnaissance air photograph taken on 8 April 1917 had also shown a square 'platform' feature in the base of the crater which could have been the covering for a shaft down to the system. After clearing the undergrowth the two most likely areas on the west side of the crater were excavated down to a depth of 2m; the maximum possible without revetting being put in place above the excavations to prevent slippage. Unfortunately no sign of the entrance

Remains of a German soldier and a cross and rosary which was found clutched in his left hand.

was discovered; either because the Group was digging in the wrong place or because the ground cover is deeper than anticipated.

Nevertheless during these excavations the Group did recover the remains of 2 German soldiers. The first body was located in a shell scrape next to what was believed to be the entrance to a dugout close to the south-eastern edge of the square platform. The body was partially disarticulated in that the head and limbs were separate from the torso, which was largely intact. It is assessed that he was killed and buried only to be exposed, probably by artillery fire. His partially decayed body, now in several pieces, was then hastily reburied in a shallow scrape outside the dugout entrance. From dental wear and bone growth it was possible to estimate the age of the man as around 19. Fragments of uniform, including tunic buttons, suggested that he was an ordinary infantryman. A large shrapnel fragment was found embedded in his spine and it is likely that this was what killed him.

The second body was probably that of a Gefreiter. He was aged about 22 and was found half way up the crater side between the two probable dugouts. He had been hit by artillery fire as another large metal shard was found embedded in the area of his pelvis; almost certainly a fatal injury. An area of obvious burning around the body suggested that his body had also been burnt although whether this was pre or post-mortem is unclear. What was clear was that the man had died in great pain; praying to his God as the excavators found a rosary clasped in his left hand; a poignant reminder of the human cost of war. As this article goes to press the team have just gained access to Tunnel No.19 and are about to explore the German system.

BIBLIOGRAPHY

The Durand Group (For Historical Research into Subterranean Military Activities). Constitution, 1998.

Dolamore MBE, Lieutenant Colonel Mike. Mine Warfare on the Western Front 1914 - 1918. (RLC Review 2003).

Dolamore MBE, Lieutenant Colonel Mike. Mine Warfare on the Western Front 1914-1918; Technical Investigation of the P73G3 Camouflet Mine and Goodman Subway at Vimy Ridge. (IofEE, November 2002).

Dolamore MBE, Lieutenant Colonel Mike. Mine Warfare on the Western Front 1914-1918 Part2: Conquering the 'O' Sector Deep Defensive Mine System at Vimy Ridge. (IofEE, June 2003).

Dolamore MBE, Lieutenant Colonel Mike. Mine Warfare on the Western Front 1914-1918; History, Principles and Design. (IofEE, December 2003).

Grieve, Captain W. Grant & Newman, Bernard. Tunnellers. The Story of the Tunnelling Companies, Royal Engineers, during the Great War. (London, Herbert Jenkins Limited, 1936), pp. 26-29.

This was approximately the maximum continuous length of the Western Front manned by the British Army during 1916-17 and stretched from north of Ypres in Flanders down to the region around the River Somme in France.

Barrie, Alexander. War Underground. (London, Tom Donovan, 1961).

Passingham, Ian. Pillars of Fire, The Battle for Messines Ridge June 1917. (Stroud, Sutton Publishing, 1998), p. 162.

S.S. 115. Notes on Mining (Translated from the French). General Staff, June 1916. The National Archives WO 158/130.

Acknowledgments to Nick Pryor for his preliminary research on the P73G3 camouflet mine.

A typical defensive mining system consisted of a number of shafts or inclines (normally at least 2 and sometimes as many as 9/10) driven down to the required depth (typically between 60 - 80 feet but sometimes exceeding 100 feet) where the tunnels branched right and left and joined up to form a main lateral running parallel with, and just in front of, the main front line.

Taken from Grieve and Newman (1936) p.p. 177-178

Watkins MBE, Lieutenant Colonel Mike. Technical Investigation and Neutralisation of the Durand Mine in the Canadian memorial park, Vimy Ridge, Artois, France. D/DLSA/MKW/04 LSA 2 dated 26 Feb 98.

A small bag containing the electric detonators and 1oz explosive primers used to used to detonate the main charge.

Dolamore MBE. Lieutenant Colonel Mike. Technical Investigation and Neutralisation of the P73G3 Camouflet Mine Charge April 2000. (Durand Group 2003).

Report of Gas Poisoning Incident in O.64.D 21 August 1916 by Capt Hogan RAMC - attached to 175 Tunnelling Company War Diary, PRO 95/404.

Plate XIX of the RE Experimental Handbook, 1917.

Dolamore MBE, Lieutenant Colonel Mike. Report on the Access and Investigation of the 'O' Sector Deep Defensive Mining System, Canadian National Vimy Memorial Site March 2000 - July 2003. (Durand Group 2004).

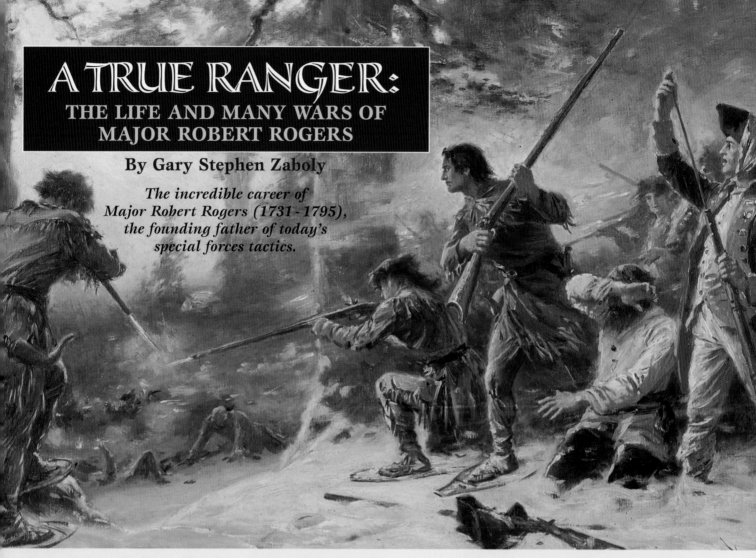

A TRUE RANGER:
THE LIFE AND MANY WARS OF MAJOR ROBERT ROGERS

By Gary Stephen Zaboly

The incredible career of
Major Robert Rogers (1731-1795),
the founding father of today's
special forces tactics.

The American frontier in the 1730s was a dangerous place to be. Life was hard for white settlers and marauding Indians would as soon scalp as trade with them. Into this harsh environment was born Robert Rogers, a boy who would grow up to be a brilliant leader of men and become one of the most charismatic, if flawed characters of his era.

Over the course of his colourful career, Rogers was a frontiersman, farmer, trapper, Ranger leader, Indian fighter (and friend), speculator, merchant, London socialite and commandant of the most important fur trading post in the West of the 1760s. It was during the French and Indian War that he set down the Rangers' "Standing Orders" on survival and guerilla warfare which were to prove his lasting legacy and are still used by US special forces today.

He also fraternised with the highest ranking officers of the British Army in North America and was twice received at Court in England. And, as if all this weren't enough, he launched a search for the elusive Northwest Passage (*as immortalized in the film of that name starring Spencer Tracy*) but his many successes were often counterbalanced, and sometimes ruined, by a variety of personal challenges that seemed to be always nipping at his heels.

This remarkable man, who ended his years in penury in London, is as little understood today as he was in his own time and has long deserved a comprehensive and fair biography. Gary Zaboly's minutely researched book seeks to remedy this omission, presenting a dispassionate and accurate account of Rogers' rollercoaster life, without recourse to moral judgment.

The book measures 11¾" x 8¼" and extends to 524 pages, including illustrative maps and photographs. It is a hard-backed volume, bound in imitation leather with gold-blocked titles, and has a full-colour dust cover. It combines the enduring qualities of a serious historical record with a thundering good read and is highly likely to become a collector's item.

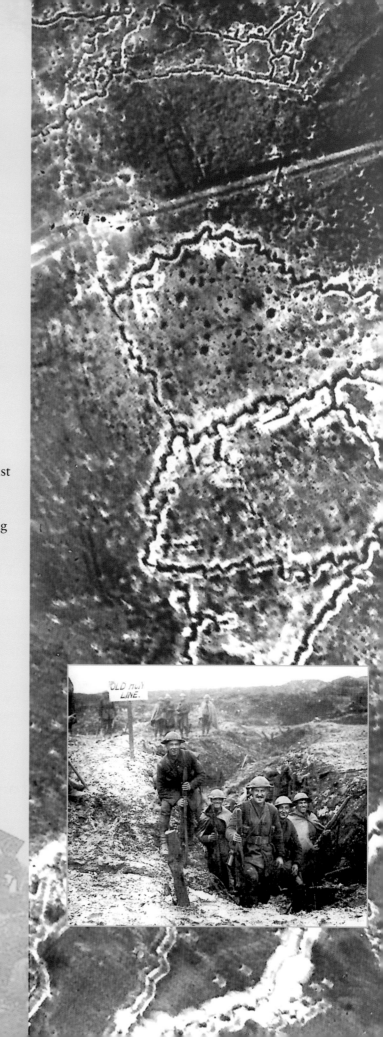

We'd found an old Boche dug-out, and he knew,
And gave us hell, for shell on frantic shell
Hammered on top, but never quite burst through.
Rain, guttering down in waterfalls of slime
Kept slush waist high, that rising hour by hour,
Choked up the steps too thick with clay to climb.
What murk of air remained stank old, and sour
With fumes of whizz-bangs, and the smell of men
Who'd lived there years, and left their curse in the den,
If not their corpses. . . .
                              There we herded from the blast
Of whizz-bangs, but one found our door at last.
Buffeting eyes and breath, snuffing the candles.
And thud! flump! thud! down the steep steps came thumping
And splashing in the flood, deluging muck —
The sentry's body; then his rifle, handles
Of old Boche bombs, and mud in ruck on ruck.
We dredged him up, for killed, until he whined
"O sir, my eyes — I'm blind — I'm blind, I'm blind!"
Coaxing, I held a flame against his lids
And said if he could see the least blurred light
He was not blind; in time he'd get all right.
"I can't," he sobbed. Eyeballs, huge-bulged like squids
Watch my dreams still; but I forgot him there
In posting next for duty, and sending a scout
To beg a stretcher somewhere, and floundering about
To other posts under the shrieking air.

Those other wretches, how they bled and spewed,
And one who would have drowned himself for good, —
I try not to remember these things now.
Let dread hark back for one word only: how
Half-listening to that sentry's moans and jumps,
And the wild chattering of his broken teeth,
Renewed most horribly whenever crumps
Pummelled the roof and slogged the air beneath —
Through the dense din, I say, we heard him shout
"I see your lights!" But ours had long died out.

'THE SENTRY' - WILFRED OWEN

HELL IN THE HEIDENKOPF

In the Spring of 2003, Andy Robertshaw, Education Officer at the National Army Museum in Chelsea, received an email from a colleague involved in the archaeology of the Great War on the Western Front. The BBC, it read, were considering sponsoring an investigation of a site near the village of Serre on the Somme battlefield as one in the series 'Ancestors' - formerly 'Meet the Ancestors'- and would involve following Peter Owen, the nephew of the famous soldier poet Wilfred Owen, in an exploration of the sites associated with his uncle's military career and poetry. Specifically the programme was intended to locate the site of a German dug-out in which Wilfred had sheltered for nearly three days in January 1917, the experience of which inspired him to write the famous poem 'The Sentry'. What followed was an extraordinary archaeological journey which, although failing in its ultimate objective, nevertheless led to results that no one on the team could have imagined.

By Andy Robertshaw

FOR SEVEN YEARS PRIOR to the start of the Owen project, I had acted as coordinator for a group of archaeologists and historians who had spent a great deal of time investigating a British trench system at Auchonvillers only a few kilometres from the proposed site near Serre. It was evident that this team had considerable experience not only in relevant archaeological techniques, but also in the background research necessary to identify both the site and the finds. The team, twelve in all, included myself as coordinator, archaeologists from UCL, Dublin, Newcastle and Belgium plus Peter Chasseaud a world-renowned map and aerial photograph expert. The entire group would have just six days to attempt the exploration of the site with a task of locating the dug-out if possible but also the exploration and recording of the trench system and associated features. On site we had assistance from Colonel Phillip Robinson of the Durand Group who has considerable experience of the exploration of both mines and dug-outs on the Western Front. Phillip arranged for the services of two EOD (Explosive Ordnance Device) experts, a vital precaution on any

'Much of the first day was taken up by a discussion between the historians as to where to commence the excavation.'

modern battlefield project, and the valuable assistance of Norbert Kruger, a German historian with access to the archives in Stuttgart.

'NOT AT THE FRONT, BUT IN FRONT OF IT'

Because of the nature of the project no prior survey work on the proposed site was carried out and the team arrived, to be filmed discussing a variety of possible locations for the trench and associated features. Much of the first day was taken up by a discussion between the historians as to where to commence the excavation. This was an important feature of the programme and involved a great deal of consulting trench maps and aerial photographs. During this time the archaeologists, EOD men and the JCB stood idle. This wasted a day although the team spent time setting up the tent and fitting out the adjacent Chapel which the Mayor of Serre had made available for secure storage. As the time taken indicated, the site for the exploration was not easy to identify because it depended upon a number of factors, many of which were interrelated. In a letter written to his mother Susan on 16th January 1917, Owen describes how he has spent the previous three days not '...*at the front, but in front of it. I held an advanced post, that is a dug-out in the middle of No Man's Land*'. At some point during

*A German
observation post
in action. It was a
dug-out such as this that
Owen held for three days in 1917.*

sniper plates, barbed wire and munitions in abundance. The entrance to one of the German mines blown on 1st July was located and the trench, which was rebuilt several times during its existence, was plotted. But the exact location of Owen's dug-out remained elusive and the discovery of three sets of human remains slowed progress in the time available.

The first set of remains found on the first day of excavation belonged to a German other rank. Wearing a set of equipment still full with ammunition he was a battlefield burial on the trench parados, who had been wrapped in his ground sheet and placed in a shell hole. Shrapnel balls were found embedded in his equipment and it was suggested at the time that this might have been the cause of death. Although his skull had been removed by plough action, fortunately his corroded ID disc was in place. The painstaking process of researching the identity of this man is discussed below.

The second soldier found was a British other rank of the King's Own (Royal Lancaster) Regiment. He was found next to a silent picket which may have been meant as a grave marker. The soldier had received terrible injuries from shell fragments. With the exception of some small denomination coins and a few personal items such as candles, only his shoulder title remained to identify him. The only battalion of his regiment that was in this location at any time in the war was 1st King's Own, 4th Division. The battalion penetrated into the Heidenkopf position on 1st July 1916 so we could at least state the date of death. However, as he was one of over 80 men who were posted as missing on that day there was little that could be done to provide more

Due to the ferocity of trench warfare, many dead soldiers could not be recovered from No Man's Land. This meant men like this British soldier were left for months, even years before they could be found, thousands never were.

this period, when Owen was sheltering from the enemy with twenty-five of his men in steadily rising water, a German shell burst in the dug-out entrance and blinded the sentry posted half way down the steps.

Although we knew, roughly, where the front line had been in January 1917 it was this dug-out that puzzled the team. The position had previously been part of the German trench system called the Heidenkopf which had stuck out towards the British Front Line. With the arrival of Norbert Kruger who brought maps from the archive in Stuttgart it was possible to locate the system of German dug-outs. These were meant to house eight men comfortably, but a quick experiment on the surface proved that twenty-five men, standing, would fit. Although there were a number of such positions it was possible to eliminate those that faced the wrong way. For a shell to burst in the entrance and injure a man half way down the steps the entrance had to face towards the German lines. This drew our attention to two areas in the front face of the Heidenkopf and it was in this area that work commenced. The initial excavation through the plough soil was done with a digger but everything else was dug by hand.

HUMAN REMAINS

Throughout the work every feature and artefact was recorded, filmed and photographed and plotted onto a master map. Over six days of work the team was able to locate the German front line trench which showed extensive damage from both man and nature. The site was very muddy and although this delayed progress it meant that organic survival was good. Trench mats and revetting survived virtually intact and the site produced

information. A coin found on the man suggested a possible connection with the Channel Islands but despite extensive research no convincing candidate has been identified. The single vulcanized fibre ID disc, which he would have been wearing, was either taken by his comrades or had rotted away. He was formally reburied by men of his Regiment on 21st April 2004.

The third casualty was also German; a senior NCO from a Württemberg unit. He was laid on his side and still had his bread bag and pocket contents including a watch stopped at 6.10, a Neolithic flint, coins and a book. The book has been partially conserved and efforts to identify this soldier are progressing well. We are confident that further research will confirm his identity.

ELUSIVE

Ultimately Owen's dug-out remained undiscovered and we have plans to return at a later date to conduct a full survey of the site. A recent collapse in the field may yet be the elusive entrance and demonstrates how close we were. What the excavation proved was the value of a carefully controlled archaeological study in which nothing was disturbed that could not be recorded. The identification of one out of three sets of human remains demonstrates the importance of having full scientific and research backup available and that even after 90 years, men can still be identified. It requires little imagination to realise what this meant to the son of Jakob Hönes, the German whose identity was recovered.

One aspect of the study, which is vitally important for students of the Great War, is the clear indication that trench maps, however accurate they might appear, are at best representational and cannot be relied upon to identify a feature on the ground. At the same time aerial photographs, which would appear to offer a better level of accuracy, only show the system of trenches that existed when the photograph was taken. As our work at Serre demonstrated, trench systems are dynamic features which are extended, destroyed, improved and realigned. A line on a map cannot be relied upon and allowances have to be made for not only the date, but also weather, combat damage and the three dimensional nature of a trench system to take into account dug-outs, tunnels and mines.

FINDING JAKOB

Shortly after the excavation at Serre had finished copies of the find sheets, as well as photographs of the bodies during excavation, including images of the identity disc and the pot lid found with the remains of the first German, were passed to Alastair Fraser historian with the No Man's Land team. The quest to find the identity of the man known simply as 'German No.1' was now on. It was a quest which would first take the research team to Germany and eventually across the Atlantic before the true story of the lost German soldier could finally be told.

By Alastair Fraser, historian

IT SEEMS IRONIC THAT THE IDENTIFICATION of the first German soldier found at Serre was carried out by a group of four researchers who were not actually present at the excavation and who have never met each other. The group initially comprised myself in England and Volker Hartmann in Germany. Additionally contact was made with Ralph Whitehead in the United States and Alexander Brunotte in Germany. Paul Blackett in England assisted with the more obscure points of the uniforms of the Imperial German Army. Communication was almost entirely by email. However, we believe that the process adopted is worthy of notice as offering a useful methodology for future cases of this nature.

29

ERKENNUNGSMARKE

Initially it was the identity disc or Erkennungsmarke which seemed to offer the quickest method to identify the man but it was badly corroded. Some of the stamped detail was still legible and showed that the man was in 7 Kompanie of a reserve infantry regiment although we could not say which one. The disc was identifiable as an early pattern issued from the beginning of the war until approximately September 1915, although they were in use after that time. These discs gave the type and number of the regiment, the company in which the owner was serving and his number on the company roll. A cause of concern to many soldiers was that the disc did not give the man's name. Any fatal casualty who was not buried by his immediate comrades obviously stood a good chance of finding an anonymous grave if the disc was the only means of identification. The new pattern disc gave the name and address to avoid this. Our man was clearly bothered by this situation as he had rather inexpertly scratched some writing on the reverse of the disc but because of the corrosion it was very difficult to make much sense of this. The writing was in three lines. Volker Hartmann is a librarian in Germany and is familiar with the Sutterlin script. He suggested the following reading:

'Mun …'

'Hines'

'Jak …'

The meaning was difficult to determine. The first line might be part of a surname or a place name; the second

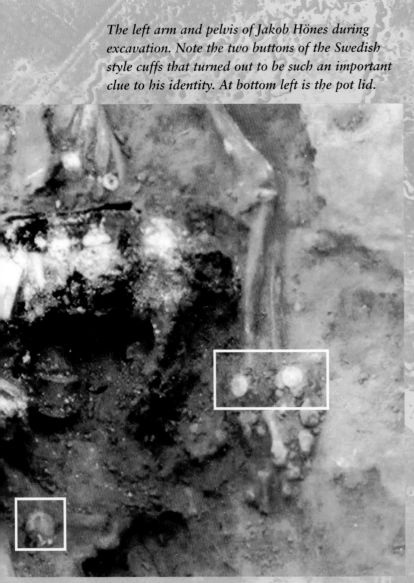

The left arm and pelvis of Jakob Hönes during excavation. Note the two buttons of the Swedish style cuffs that turned out to be such an important clue to his identity. At bottom left is the pot lid.

The position of the body on the parados of a German trench, probably having been hoisted out of the trench wrapped in his groundsheet.

Front of the badly corroded identity disc with the fragmentary regimental and company identification.

The reverse of the identity disc with the cryptic text scratched on it, demonstrating the difficulty of getting a meaningful reading.

line did not seem to make any sense and was not a known German surname. The word appeared to be complete whatever it meant; the third line could be part of a Christian name, a surname, a place name or part of an address. It was fairly clear that we could not expect an immediate solution from this source without carefully examining the other clues on the body and also looking at German military histories to establish a detailed order of battle which might enable us to eliminate some units from our enquiries. There were a number of features both in the uniform and equipment and the personal items that could help in the identification process. We could check our deductions against the historical sources to see if they were plausible. An important priority was to narrow down the possible date of death. From this information we might be able to find a 7 *Kompanie* of a reserve infantry regiment that was known to have been in the *Heidenkopf* position at a time consistent with the dating evidence on the body. We might then be able to approach the formidable task of finding casualty lists for the most likely regiment or regiments.

COMPLEX SYSTEM

We were aware that the Imperial German Army began the Great War with a very complex system of identifying regiments by various uniform details. Much of this system relied upon different coloured piping,

'We were aware that the Imperial German Army began the Great War with a very complex system of identifying regiments by various uniform details.'

embroidered monograms and numerals, and lace on collars or shoulder straps. The situation was further complicated by the fact that the identification system did not long survive the outbreak of war. New regiments were often formed from companies of several other regiments and might retain their distinctions until issued with new uniforms. For security reasons identifying features were often removed from uniforms and, as the Germans suffered from a shortage of uniforms, items of clothing recovered from casualties were often reissued.

Despite the fact that virtually no fabric has survived from the uniform we were able to make a number of significant deductions from the arrangement of the buttons and other tunic fittings which had survived. The tunic buttons were of the standard Prussian type bearing a crown, which should, in theory, have eliminated troops from other states. However the individual was wearing a leather belt with a Bavarian buckle of an early pattern, which could potentially have confused the issue. During 1915 Bavarian troops began to be issued with tunics bearing Prussian buttons so it was possible the body was that of a Bavarian soldier. An extensive search of the available German printed histories failed to turn up any Bavarian units in the *Heidenkopf* area at any stage of the war and we had to conclude tentatively that the man had acquired the belt as a souvenir, either during pre-war service or earlier on in the war. The cartridge pouches associated with the belt were of the M1895 pattern and were filled with 10 chargers of 7.92 mm rounds. The head stamps on the rounds were dated between 1911 and 1913. This was consistent with an early date for the casualty. M1895 pouches were obsolete by 1914 but were commonly issued to reservists on mobilisation and this was consistent with his known status as a member of a reserve regiment.

The position of the buttons and hooks on the tunic showed that the man was wearing an M1910 *Waffenrock* tunic which suggested a 1914 or 1915 date, although this type was in use throughout the war. A significant clue was the arrangement of the buttons on the cuffs. These comprised two buttons parallel to the cuff turn-back which indicated that they were of the Swedish pattern rather than the commoner Brandenburg type. The area was occupied by *1* and *2 Garde Division* from October 1914 to March 1915. German Guard infantry had distinctive lace decoration on their tunics which should have survived. As none was present it seemed more likely that the man served in a regiment of *26 Reserve Division*, a formation from *Württemberg*, which was in the area from March 1915 to early November 1916. Examination of works on Imperial German Army uniforms revealed that, although Swedish cuffs were common in the Württemberg army, only one regiment in 26 Reserve Division wore them. This was *121 Reserve Infanterie* Regiment. This unit has an excellent printed history which contained a photograph showing men in M1910 tunics wearing M1895 pattern ammunition pouches. Clothing took a lot of punishment over the winter of 1915-16 and many men were issued with the M1915 pattern *Bluse* in the spring of 1916, which suggested our man might be a 1915 casualty. In addition we knew from the regimental history that *7 Kompanie, 121 RIR* took part in the defence of the trenches south west of Serre during the French offensive of June 1915. Fighting here was heavy and confused, exactly the situation in which the dead might not have been recovered.

A NAME...AND A FACE

The personal items found in the man's bread bag were not of any help in identification although they were a poignant reminder of his humanity. They included a comb, a spoon, a broken mirror, a nail cleaner and the remains of an indelible pencil. A very significant find was a glass pot lid with a readable printed surface. This had been in the right trouser pocket. The legend on the

The pot lid from the firm of Edouard Breuninger in Stuttgart which confirmed that the soldier must have come from Württemberg.

lid read 'E. Breuninger zum Grossfürsten. Münzstrasse Stuttgart Sporerstr. Aussteuer-Waren, Putz-Artikel, Pelze, Gardinen, Teppiche. Damen-,Herren- u, Kinder-Konfektion. Manufacturwaren, Besätze.' Volker Hartmann was able to trace the firm of Eduard Breuninger which is still trading in Stuttgart, although not at the same address as in 1914. The firm was a fairly substantial operation at that time with several department stores in central Germany. They suggested that the pot had contained shoe polish or dubbin. The list of items that the store sold translates as 'Trousseau, cleaning goods, furs, net curtains, Ladies', gentlemen's and childrens' ready to wear clothes. Textiles, trimmings'. The lid also gave us independent confirmation that German No. 1 had come from the correct area to be a member of *121 RIR* which was composed of men from the Heilbronn and Ludwigsburg area, north of Stuttgart.

At this point we had a reasonable case to be able to state that the body was that of a soldier from 7 *Kompanie* of *121 Reserve Infanterie Regiment* and that he might have been killed about 13th June 1915. Unfortunately the printed history of the regiment did not contain a list of non-commissioned casualties and we had little prospect of getting to the *Hauptstaatsarchiv* in Stuttgart where we might have found such lists. At that point I posted a request for help on the Great War Forum on the Internet and made contact with Ralph Whitehead, a researcher living in Fayetteville, New York. Ralph has been researching the units of *XIV Armee Korps*, which served on the Somme from 1914 to

1916. He was able to produce a list of the casualties of *121* and *119 RIR*. *119 RIR* served in the same area and it was possible, although less likely, that our man could be from this regiment. Examination of the lists for 7 *Kompanie*, *121 RIR* produced a Jakob Hönes who was killed on 13th June 1915. On looking at the identity disc we could see an umlaut over the 'i' of 'Hines' and realised that it was in fact an 'o'. We learned from Ralph Whitehead that Hönes came from the village of Münchingen which is north west of Stuttgart. This information fitted exactly with the scratched writing on the identity disc which now read in full:

'*Münchingen*'
'*Hönes*'
'*Jakob*'

As we now had a name for German No. 1 we were able to make a start on finding further details of his life and career. Volker Hartmann contacted the archives in Münchingen and received invaluable help from the archivist, Alexander Brunotte, who not only provided information from the town records but has also visited the Hauptstaatsarchiv in Stuttgart which houses the war diaries and personnel records of *121 RIR*. Alexander Brunotte also contacted Jakob Hönes' family, many of whom still lived in Münchingen. Astonishingly Ernst Christian Hönes, one of Jakob's six children, was still alive aged 93. He was only 4 when his father went off to war and would not have remembered him. He died in 2004 knowing that his father had been found and would be assured an honourable burial amongst his comrades. Whilst the No Man's Land team were excavating at Auchonvillers in April 2004 Volker Hartmann emailed us a postcard of a group of German soldiers which included Jakob Hönes. Our involvement with him had begun with a group of anonymous bones to which, after five months of painstaking work, we had been able to put an identity; it was very moving, finally, to look at his face.

Jakob Hönes with the men of his Korporalschaft, a group of about 16 men, equivalent to half a platoon. The photograph was probably taken in early April 1915. Jakob is the man lying in the front row on the left of the group. The man in the row above and to the right with the Iron Cross 2nd Class ribbon may be his brother Christian. Note the mixture of cuff styles with both Brandenburg and Swedish cuffs, showing the different uniform types to be found within one unit.

A LIFE

From material in the *Hauptstaatsarchiv* in Stuttgart, the town archives of Münchingen and the published regimental and divisional histories, much of it assembled by Alexander Brunotte, it is possible to produce a very full biography of Jakob Hönes, a man who has probably become more widely known in death than he ever was in life. He was born in Münchingen on 9th December 1880, the eldest son of Georg and Christiane Sofie Hönes. His father was a farmer who had got into financial trouble through unsuccessful trading in horses. The

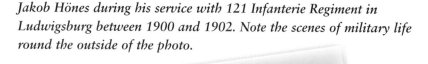

'Military service was seen as a 'rite of passage', from which one emerged as a man.'

family had four other children, Karl Christian, Friedrike, Christian and a daughter, Sofie, who died at the age of two. Jakob's mother died when he was young and his father remarried. There was another child of this marriage named Wilhelm.

Jakob attended the local *Volkschule* from 1887 until he was 14. There is no record of him attending any other school and he probably worked on his father's farm. He attended the archaic ceremony of paying homage to the King of Württemberg, Wilhelm II, at the village hall in 1898, for which he received 50 pfennigs. In 1900 Jakob became liable for military service. Germany was a highly militarised society at that time and the army was a familiar and respected institution. There was a large depot at Ludwigsburg, a short distance north of Münchingen and the fields near the village were often used for large-scale manoeuvres.

Military service was seen as a 'rite of passage', from which one emerged as a man. After passing the medical examination the young men of Münchingen put on their best suits and hats and paraded around the village with beer mugs in hand. A horse drawn cart, decorated with boughs and ribbons, accompanied them on their progress. Jakob Hönes served with *121 Infanterie Regiment* or to give it its full title *Infanterie-Regiment Alt-Württemberg (3. Württembergisches) Nr.121*. They were based in the garrison town of Ludwigsburg and the regiment had a long and illustrious history, having been formed in March 1716. It had fought in the Napoleonic Wars, the Austro-Prussian War of 1866 and the Franco-Prussian War. On completion of his training Jakob had his photo taken in uniform when he left the army in 1902.

Jakob is normally described as a day labourer or groom, a fairly menial station in society. Münchingen was a village of some 1,500 people which had relatively few prosperous farmers or minor gentry. The rest of the population owned small farms or were landless and life for these people was undoubtedly hard. In 1906 the village was connected to Stuttgart by railway so that it was possible for villagers to commute to factories in the city. It also made the transport of farm produce much easier. Jakob appears to have worked for a number of

Jakob Hönes during his service with 121 Infanterie Regiment in Ludwigsburg between 1900 and 1902. Note the scenes of military life round the outside of the photo.

Jakob and Marie Hönes. The drawn in tunic is somewhat strange but the photo may have been taken in 1908 when they were married.

village now had electricity and running water and the Hönes family must have enjoyed a reasonable standard of living. Sadly events in the Balkans in the summer of 1914 were to destroy their happiness and that of millions of others like them throughout Europe.

WAR AND TREPIDATION

There appears to have been relatively little enthusiasm for the war in rural Württemberg, in contrast to the scenes of joy displayed in towns and cities throughout Germany. Life in the countryside was hard enough without the added problems of the young men disappearing into the army just as the harvest was due. Jakob Hönes went off to war on 6th August 1914, never to return, leaving a pregnant wife, a teenage stepson and four young children under the age of 6. It was a prospect no father could have viewed with anything other than trepidation. Jakob joined the newly formed *121 Reserve Infanterie Regiment* with the rank of *Wehrmann*. The regiment was part of *26 Reserve Division*, a Württemberg formation of five infantry regiments with artillery, medical personnel, pioneers, a bridging

employers, perhaps on a seasonal basis. In 1906 he was employed in the local brickworks and the following year he was a farmhand on an estate producing sugar beet for *Zuckerfabrik Stuttgart*, a sugar company. It was possibly during this job that he got to know Marie Ansel from the neighbouring village of Hirschlanden. Two of her relatives are known to have worked as servants on the estate. In 1908 he and Marie were married. Marie had a 7 year-old son from her first marriage. A photograph shows the couple, probably at this time. Jakob is wearing his army uniform, very likely the smartest clothes he possessed. After a period in the reserve Jakob was transferred to the *Landwehr* which required two annual periods of training to be undertaken each year to keep men's skills up to date.

In 1911 Jakob was working for a bricklayer but was able to buy a small house in Münchingen, perhaps with money his wife had brought into the marriage. The house had three rooms, a kitchen, cellar and pigsty. In addition Jakob was able to obtain a small piece of land. Between 1908 and 1914 Jakob and Marie had four children. The

> 'Jakob Hönes went off to war on 6th August 1914, never to return...'

German lorries transporting men up to the Front in the Bapaume region.

train, field bakeries and all the other ancillary troops necessary to sustain it.

On 3rd September *Wehrmann* Jakob Hönes was posted to 7 *Kompanie* of the second battalion, which was raised in Heilbronn under the command of Major Otto Bürger. Jakob served with the regiment in the fighting against the French in the Nancy and Epinal areas. On 23rd September the regiment entrained for a move northwards with the rest of the *26 Reserve Division* as the Germans attempted to outflank the French. The division unloaded in the Cambrai area and marched down towards Albert, over what was to become the battlefield of the Somme. There was particularly heavy fighting during a night action near Thiepval on 28th/29th September in which 20 men were killed, 212 wounded and no less than 80 men unaccounted for. Major Bürger, Jakob's battalion commander, was wounded by a rifle bullet. The neighbouring division at this period was a Bavarian one and could be the source of the belt found on Jakob's body. Mobile warfare ceased and both sides dug in; *121 RIR* were allocated a sector running from the south of Thiepval village to the fortification known as the *Wundt-Werk*.

AN DER SOMME

As the year drew on and the weather deteriorated, conditions became difficult in the trenches. Jakob's battalion spent Christmas in the line, a time that must have been particularly depressing for him as Marie had just given birth to a daughter Luise, a child he was never to see. His brother Christian was recovering from wounds in Ludwigsburg and was probably able to visit his new niece. There was no Christmas truce with the French unlike the friendly scenes further north between the British and Germans. When out of the line the battalion was able to rest in the villages of Courcelette and Miraumont which were equipped with baths, reading rooms with the latest papers and magazines and even German pubs. Damage to the rear areas at this time was very light compared to the devastation wrought upon on them by the British in 1916. The food issued to the troops was reasonable in quantity and quality compared to later in the war when food shortages began to bite seriously. The men were given 'meat, mostly fresh, and vegetables. In addition they were given bacon, sausages, cheese and eggs. Alcohol was handed out daily in the form of rum and cognac in tea or coffee, milk every four days, beer and wine every now and then'.

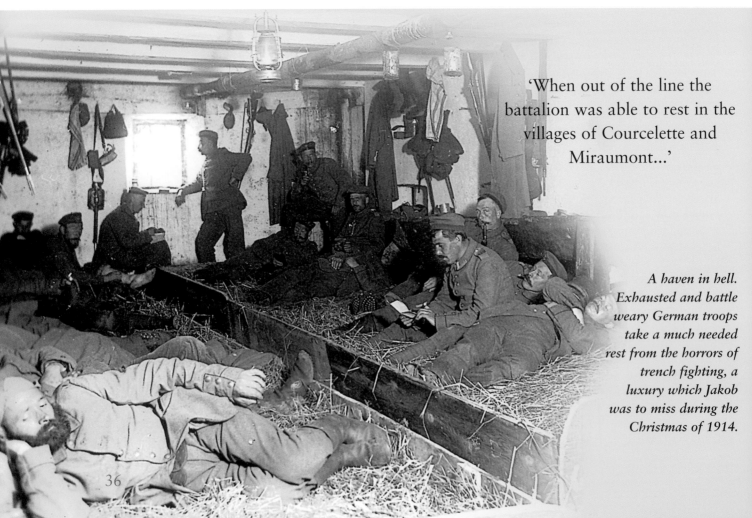

'When out of the line the battalion was able to rest in the villages of Courcelette and Miraumont...'

A haven in hell. Exhausted and battle weary German troops take a much needed rest from the horrors of trench fighting, a luxury which Jakob was to miss during the Christmas of 1914.

The poor weather conditions only added to the misery of the fear, home-sickness, injury and death experienced by soldiers in the trenches.

Each company had a well-stocked canteen where combs, writing paper, cheese, oranges, and even beer and wine were on sale. Access to alcohol in the German Army seems to have been much less strictly controlled than in the British Army, despite the fact that German soldiers were traditionally heavy beer drinkers. They tended to favour cigars and pipes rather than cigarettes like the British. There was also a divisional photographer who was employed to take individual or group photographs and it is probably from this source that the photo of Jakob Hönes and his comrades originated.

In March *II/121 RIR* was moved to occupy a stretch of front line near Ovillers on the division's southern boundary. One consolation was that his younger brother Christian was transferred to 7 *Kompanie* on 2nd April 1915.

Three postcards, written by Jakob, survive from this period. He seems not to have been particularly at ease with writing. His style is somewhat archaic and there are a number of Schwabian dialect words in evidence, perhaps not surprising for a man who had had a minimum of education. The content is very mundane and he was principally concerned with 6 marks that he has sent to his wife which she did not seem to have received. He also expressed the hope that the major part of the war must by now be over and poignantly he ends one card:

> '*Meanwhile a kiss and greetings from your dear husband Jakob, dear Marie, and from your dear father, dear children Albert, Emma, Eugen, little Ernst, Sophie and Luise. Goodbye. Forget me not.*'

At the time that he wrote this Jakob Hönes had just over seven weeks to live.

FRENCH OFFENSIVE

By early June it was clear that the French were planning a major offensive in the area of Serre with the intention of retaking that village, which occupied a commanding height that would have overlooked the German lines for some distance. Artillery fire increased to previously unheard of levels of intensity in the sector

Disease was yet another enemy to fight on the frontline. Like these men, Jakob would have received an inoculation injection against typhus during his time in the trenches.

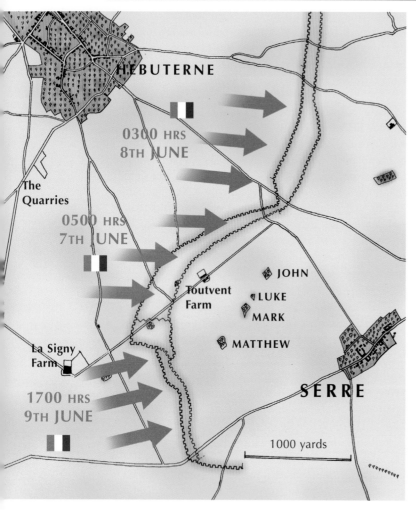

Three separate French attacks on the German Line.

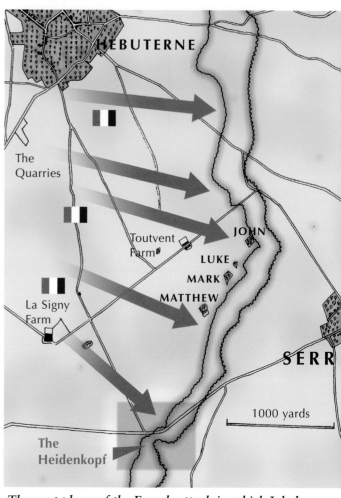

The next phase of the French attack in which Jakob was killed. This assault eliminated the German strongholds in front of Serre.

occupied by the division to the north and the French were seen to be cutting gaps in their own wire, a sure sign of an impending infantry attack. *II/121 RIR* was actually out of the line when the French assault began on the morning of 7th June 1915, 7 *Kompanie* being at Miraumont. The regimental staff went to their battle headquarters and 7 and 8 *Kompanie* were moved nearer the front line to Artillerie Mulde or Artillery Valley just to the north of Beaumont, ready to be called forward as reinforcements. A counter-attack planned for the evening of 7th June was called off before it began although some casualties were suffered from artillery fire. Instead the other two companies were

On the morning of 13th June it reached a peak and the sentries announced 'The French are coming!'

brought over the Ancre from Courcelette and the entire battalion concentrated in the valley. It was very likely at this time that Jakob was issued with the ammunition found in his pouches.

Over the next couple of days the companies were committed to the front line to shore up the German positions south west of Serre which were now the focus of furious French attacks. 7 *Kompanie* was the last one to move and was positioned to the east of the Serre to Mailly-Maillet road, just to the north of what is now Serre Road No. 2 British cemetery. Much of the original German front line was now in French hands and the battalion was subjected to very heavy shelling

French troops on high alert await a German counter-attack amongst battle debris after capturing an enemy trench.

for the next two days. On the morning of 13th June it reached a peak and the sentries announced *'The French are coming!'* From the north and northwest several lines of French infantry launched themselves on the German positions. The trenches to the north of the main road were overwhelmed and only four men were able to escape, having feigned death amongst the French casualties. Several others died later in French prisoner of war camps. Despite this initial success the enemy assault broke down under heavy rifle and machine gun fire from the trenches on the other side of the road. This failure

marked the end of French attempts to capture Serre. The 'heroic resistance' of *II/121* had, according to the regimental history, been responsible for the repulse. But success came at a high price. The battalion suffered 211 casualties, 81 of whom were killed, including the battalion commander Hauptmann Guido Nagel. 7 *Kompanie* lost 18 dead with 6 others missing, presumed killed.

KIA

It appears that Jakob Hönes was killed or incapacitated early on in the action as his ammunition pouches were still full, something that seems unlikely if he had participated in the defence. In the company roll he is recorded as *'killed in action at Serre near Albert, Northern France, by rifle bullet, buried close to the lines 1 km south of Serre'*. A family tradition seems to indicate that his brother Christian was with him when he died – one hopes that this was the case. A number of shell fragments were found in the pelvis area, although these could be the result of post-mortem injury. A French rifle bullet was found near the chest but is not thought to have been the projectile that killed him. The body appears to have been wrapped in a *Zeltbahn* or

'killed in action at Serre near Albert, Northern France, by rifle bullet, buried close to the lines 1 km south of Serre.'

THE COMPANY ROLL

An aerial photograph of the Heidenkopf taken July 1st 1916 before the 'Big Push'. The area boxed indicates the area Jakob's body was buried.

The funeral of Jakob Hönes and his comrade at Labry German Military Cemetery with Bundeswehr personnel in attendance.

groundsheet, the eyelets of which were found round him. He was probably slung over the parados of the trench and dragged a short distance at some time after death, his ammunition pouches having ridden up to his chest in the process. Given the extremely shallow depth at which the body was discovered burial seems to have been fairly perfunctory. The German positions were severely battered and in urgent need of consolidation; disposal of the dead would have been carried out as quickly as possible.

LOSS

Jakob's death was recorded in the company roll on 18th June 1915 by his company commander. The *Ersatz* or replacement battalion informed the town authorities in Münchingen, although it is not known how the news was broken to Marie Hönes. In the years to come life was extremely hard for her, although she was better off than many urban families. In 1917 she was even able to

buy another field but all of the children that were old enough to walk had to help out with various agricultural tasks as food became short. The loss of Jakob was not the only blow the Hönes family was to suffer during the war; Christian survived the battle for Serre with a slight wound but on 24th July 1916 he was wounded again and died at the dressing station at Miraumont. The previous month his half-brother, Wilhelm, had been killed at Hill 60 in the Ypres Salient whilst serving with *125 Infanterie Regiment*. Marie Hönes married again in the 1920s but was destined to lose a third husband, who died in a Soviet prisoner of war camp in 1947.

HONOUR

This story of a humble German *Landseer* came to a satisfactory conclusion in August 2004 when he and his as yet unidentified comrade were buried at the German military cemetery at Labry near Metz. No less than fourteen members of his family attended the funeral and Volker Hartmann represented the No Man's Land group. By coincidence a number of *Bundeswehr* soldiers were working in the cemetery and were able to provide the two men with a guard of honour. Professional excavation and patient research were vital; only in this way can we hope to give the lost soldiers of both sides a dignified and identified resting place alongside their comrades.

The team that worked on the Serre project has now become a formal Great War archaeological and historical group with the name 'No Man's Land'. No Man's Land is a multi-national group of archaeologicalists, historians and specialists actively involved in archaeological research of WWI. Formed in 2003 the group carries out an annual programme of projects on the Western Front. It has worked with European partners in investigating threatened sites and is currently involved in the production of a television documentary series to be shown in November 2005.

I am the enemy you killed, my friend.
I knew you in this dark: for so you frowned
Yesterday through me as you jabbed and killed.
I parried; but my hands were loath and cold.
Let us sleep now...

WILFRED OWEN (STRANGE MEETING 1917)

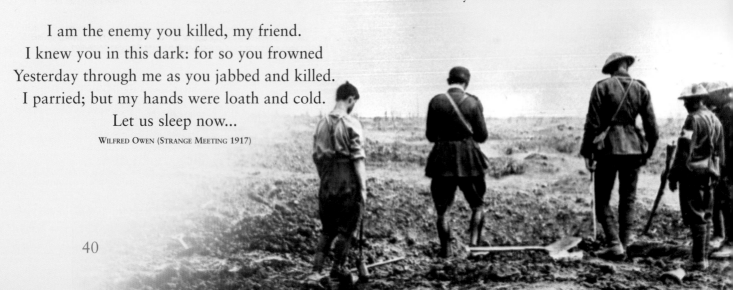

Too old to fight

Too proud to ask

This is Rifleman Lalbahadur Thapa (L) aged 93 and his younger brother Rifleman Dilbahadur Thapa. Both served with 6th Gurkha Rifles throughout World War Two.

The brothers keep each other company on the five day walk they make every three months from their home village to the nearest Gurkha Welfare Trust Area Welfare Centre to collect their 'welfare pension'. This money is the only source of income and all that stands between them and destitution.

For over 180 years the Gurkhas have helped to fight our wars and keep our peace. Gurkhas have won 13 Victoria Crosses and have served in most of the major conflicts of the 20th century.

If there was a minute's silence for every Gurkha casualty from World War Two alone, we would have to keep quiet for two whole weeks. But silence will not help the living, the wounded and disabled, those without military pensions following World War Two service or redundancy, or those left destitute by ill health or natural disasters.

There is no doubt that we in this country owe the Gurkhas a debt of honour, and the Gurkha Welfare Trust is seeking to repay that debt. The work of the Trust is now vital to the health, well-being and quality of life for thousands of Gurkha old soldiers and their dependants.

Please will you help us? Anything you can send now will be gratefully received and carefully used in relieving hardship and distress among Gurkha ex-service-men and their dependants in Nepal.

'On the royalist left
the terrain was far
more difficult, with
far more hedgerows
held by
parliamentarian
musketeers.'

THE BATTLE OF EDGEHILL: HISTORY FROM THE FIELD

On Sunday 23rd October 1642 the army of the Earl of Essex, the parliamentarian Lord General, and the army of Charles I clashed in the first major action of the Civil War in England. They fought in the open fields between the villages of Radway and Kineton in Warwickshire. The battle of Edgehill was intended to be the one great battle to decide the war. Although it is often viewed as indecisive, the king actually gained an important advantage. Essex failed to break through to the capital and had to retreat to the security of the parliamentarian garrison at Warwick, leaving Banbury and Oxford to fall to the royalists. More importantly it left the enemy in command of the road to London, and control of the capital was the key to the war. Had this advantage been exploited immediately, as Prince Rupert urged, then the Civil War might have been ended within a few days of Edgehill. Glenn Foard, professional archaeologist and Project Officer for the Battlefields Trust, reports on the latest developments in and possible consequences of the ongoing archaeological survey of this key battlefield.

By Glenn Foard

A BRIEF NARRATIVE OF THE BATTLE

Essex deployed in the open fields of Kineton, forcing the royalists to descend from the heights of Edgehill, where the army had its rendezvous that morning. Essex placed his army in a defensive formation, though the exact detail is subject to dispute. The vast majority of the parliamentarian cavalry were placed on the left wing under the command of Ramsey, covering a wide frontage to prevent the royalists outflanking them on that side. These cavalry were interlined with about 400 musketeers to provide extra firepower, while a 'forlorn hope' of about 300 musketeers were positioned along the hedgerow to the fore and to the left. Some artillery pieces were also deployed in support. Essex had clearly learned lessons from the defeat at Powick Bridge: that the royalist cavalry were a dominant force and that his cavalry should avail themselves of whatever

'The vast majority of the parliamentarian cavalry were placed on the left wing under the command of Ramsey, covering a wide frontage to prevent the royalists outflanking them on that side.'

protection the terrain offered. On the right wing Balfour was extremely weak in cavalry. This was in part because some units had not yet reached Kineton but, as we shall see later, it was also probably a response to the limitations, or opportunities, provided by the terrain. Here again Essex took advantage of the hedged enclosures that flanked the field on this side, deploying 700 dragoons to line these hedgerows to the fore, in support of Balfour. The presence of these enclosures, narrowing the frontage on that side, allowed Essex to deploy a small number of his troops of horse behind the foot. This was a decision which was to prove a key factor in the battle as it protected them from Wilmot's cavalry charge and enabled them to play a crucial role later in the action. In the centre the parliamentarian infantry were deployed in two lines according to Dutch tactics.

In the royalist battle array Rupert commanded the right wing of cavalry, where the bulk of the horse were placed, while on the royalist left Wilmot had well under 1000 horse. In the centre the infantry were deployed, according to Prince Rupert's wishes, in the more complex Swedish formation. Even with the excellent plan of the royalist deployment, drawn up some years after the battle for Rupert by de Gomme, there is still some dispute about the detail of the royalist battle array. Some reconstructions show three battalions in the front line with two in support in the second line, whereas other authors suggest five and four battalions respectively. The new book by Scott et al suggests yet another alternative for both armies. Of perhaps 1000 royalist dragoons, two regiments were on the left and one on the right wing.

After an initial artillery exchange, Rupert used dragoons to clear the enemy musketeers from the hedgerows on his right flank, allowing him to mount his all important cavalry attack. His troopers charged home without halting to fire their pistols. Having taken a highly defensive stance on the top of a slight ridge, behind hedgerows, the parliamentarian cavalry seem to have stood to take the royalist charge instead of meeting it at the charge. The royalist troopers cleared the hedgerow and burst in amongst Ramsey's men who turned and fled. The parliamentarian infantry brigade adjacent to the cavalry was also swept away, weakening Essex's position even further.

On the royalist left the terrain was far more difficult, with far more hedgerows held by parliamentarian musketeers. But again dragoons, riding to the field and then dismounting to fight on foot, were used to clear the enclosures. This allowed Wilmot's cavalry to charge, with a similar result to that achieved by Rupert on the right wing. But, as at key points in later battles during the Civil War, the royalist horse seconding both cavalry wings failed to exploit the dramatic advantage that Rupert and Wilmot had given the royalist army. Instead of turning their divisions of horse against the unprotected flanks of Essex's infantry, both Byron and Digby followed in the pursuit. The royalist horse chased the fleeing parliamentarians in a destructive execution for at least the 1.5 miles to Kineton. Some probably pursued well beyond the village but many, probably funnelled north westward by the enclosures east of Kineton, abandoned the pursuit and attacked Essex's baggage train when they reached the town. Meanwhile, on the battlefield, just a handful of horse on both sides managed to regroup in support of the infantry. In this situation Balfour's troops of parliamentarian horse, who had been protected between the infantry lines, probably just as Essex had intended, would come into their own, helping to turn back the tide of the royalist infantry advance.

As the cavalry charge went in, the royalist infantry had advanced to within musket shot and the firefight began. The parliamentarians held their position on the higher ground, the division on the left side probably protected behind the same hedgerow that Ramsey's men had used on the left wing. But Essex's infantry were immediately at a disadvantage, for in the cavalry action the front brigade on the left flank and the reserve on the right had been swept away. In response, reserve forces were quickly brought in to hold the line, as the front

Figure 1: The battlefield is seen here, just beyond Radway village in the Vale of the Red Horse, viewed from the Castle Inn on Edgehill.

lines came to push of pike. While at this stage of the war the royalists had superiority in cavalry, Essex's infantry were by far the best equipped and trained on the field. This, combined with a limited advantage in the small numbers of cavalry still on the field, enabled Essex to hold the royalists after initially being driven back. His cavalry mounted a flank attack on the royalist infantry while they were fully engaged and two of the royalist regiments were broken by the combined cavalry and infantry assault. Those not killed or captured fled back towards Edgehill. Balfour's cavalry charge carried him right through to the royalist artillery where he disabled several pieces. For a time, with support from the King's Lifeguard of Foot from the reserves, the royalist left held the combined infantry and cavalry attack, but they finally broke and ran when Balfour's cavalry also attacked from the rear. Only on the right did the royalist regiments hold their own as the centre and left fell back in disorder. The few royalist horse remaining on the field, under Lucas, attempted their own charge but were countered by other parliamentarian horse. As the light started to fade the royalists were pushed back to their artillery. But they retained their cohesion, thanks largely to the presence of a ditch which they were able to defend, and the support of very effective artillery fire. This enabled their left wing, which had given most ground, to reform.

The royalist horse, occupied in the pursuit and plundering, had eventually found themselves faced by parliamentarian reserves marching to the battle. Some of these troops, under Hampden, engaged the royalists and drove them off, but it was now too late for these fresh parliamentarian forces to influence the battle. Nor indeed could the royalist cavalry affect the outcome as they finally returned to the field, despite causing some problems for the parliamentarian infantry as they passed by. It was now too late in the day to mount any sort of offensive cavalry action. As the light failed and the powder and ammunition began to run low, the battle subsided into a stand off. The parliamentarians had pushed the royalist infantry back and apparently stood all night where the king's forces had formed their initial battle array, within musket shot of the enemy. Early that

Figure 2: The monument beside Graveyard Coppice, now within the compound of the MOD's Edgehill depot, lies close to the site of a mass grave, according to Burne. It seems likely that this was where Essex halted the initial royalist infantry advance.

morning the royalists withdrew up onto Edgehill and then the parliamentarians back towards Kineton. After dawn Essex once more drew up his army in battle array in Kineton field but the royalists had gone from Edgehill. In response Essex withdrew his men to Kineton, where they rested while the dead were buried, then marched on to Warwick.

PREVIOUS STUDIES

The standard work on Edgehill since 1967 has been that by Young, supplemented in 1995 by the English Heritage Battlefields Register report and by the local detail provided in Tennant's important study of the war in Warwickshire.[1] In addition there are a number of articles dealing with specific aspects of the battle or the armies, and several antiquarian contributions.[2] In the last three years two new books have appeared on the Battle of Edgehill.[3] Each has much to commend it for the general reader, with Roberts and Tincey for example, providing a valuable discussion of the Swedish and Dutch tactics employed by either side, while Scott et al present important new evidence on the parliamentarian casualties. Yet, like so many of the books on battles in Britain now being produced, they do not fundamentally advance understanding of the events. They do suggest interesting alternative reinterpretations of the deployments and action, but are all still based squarely on the long known documentary sources for the battle that were exploited so extensively thirty years ago by Young. If we are to make substantial advances then wholly new data must be brought to bear.

Young himself, following Burne,[4] understood that battle archaeology could assist in the interpretation of battles and here, at Edgehill in 1967, he attempted the first recorded metal detecting survey on an English battlefield, with the assistance of the Ministry of Defence. Unfortunately they had little success, recovering only a handful of artefacts, none of which could be securely associated with the action.[5] Scott et al also discuss the importance of exploring the battle archaeology and of reconstructing the historic terrain of the battlefield, yet they advance these aspects of the study little further than Young. It is true that they

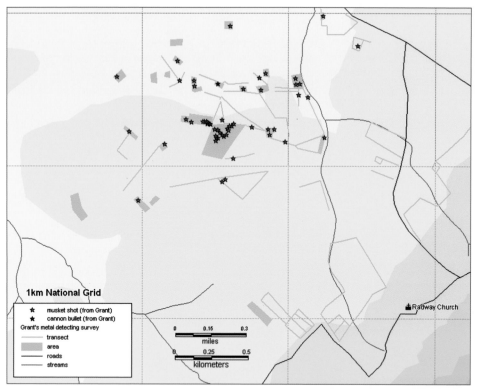

Figure 3: Captain Grant's survey of Edgehill battlefield, based on records in the Warwickshire SMR.

summarise both Walford's antiquarian records from the 19th century and Grant's metal detecting survey results of the late 1970s but the true potential of that data is not realised in their reinterpretation. In contrast, the Two Men in a Trench TV programme did carry out new work on the battle archaeology, with what appear to be useful results, particularly in the possible area of the clash over the parliamentarian baggage train, though the detailed results are as yet unpublished.

But there is other wholly unpublished work that raises serious questions about the standard interpretation of the battle. Pannet, who conducted a study of the historic map data for the region in the 1970s, realised the significance of his mapping for the interpretation of the battle. His plan of the battlefield suggests that the location and extent of the initial deployments of the two armies may have been substantially different to that suggested by Burne, Young and all subsequent authors.[6]

THE POTENTIAL OF THE BATTEFIELD

A fairly detailed picture of the battle can be built up from the wide range of documentary accounts but, as Pannet's work makes clear, there are serious questions as to the accuracy of the placing of this action within the landscape. Work at Naseby has also shown how reconstruction of the historic terrain combined with intensive metal detecting survey can enable fundamental

reinterpretation of a battle.[7] Not only at Naseby but also at Marston Moor, Cheriton and elsewhere metal detectorists have shown that there is an extensive archaeology of English battles, though their work has generally not realised the full potential of the evidence. Where such potential has been realised is in the archaeological study of battlefields in the USA, with work such as that by Scott at the Little Bighorn, Haecker on the battlefields and skirmish sites of New Mexico and Texas, Sivilich at Monmouth battlefield and Pratt at Fallen Timbers. It has long been clear that the application of such intensive systematic survey techniques to battlefields in Europe offered the potential of major advances in the understanding for sites of the mid 16th century onwards, where there are extensive scatters of lead bullets.[8]

At Edgehill the survey by Grant in the 1970s demonstrated the presence of large numbers of bullets, while the research by Two Men in a Trench has confirmed this exists over an even wider area than Grant explored.

Up to April 1979 Grant recovered 52 musket balls from the battlefield. His survey is exceptional for its time, because it includes not only apparently highly accurate mapping of finds at 1:10560 and 1:2500 scale, but also records the amount of survey time spent in each area or on each transect. This enables one to consider with his data the degree to which absence of evidence may genuinely represent evidence of absence.

Grant's survey seems to support Pannett's suggested reinterpretation of the initial deployments. His major shot concentration probably reflects the royalist initial advance and main infantry engagement in the centre. In contrast the cavalry action on the parliamentarian left wing seems to have produced almost no evidence, as one might expect, because Rupert's royalist cavalry were instructed not to stand to fire their pistols but to charge home immediately. However the absence of any evidence of the documented firing by parliamentarian musketeers on this wing might be considered surprising. But the intensity of his survey on this wing was considerably lower than in the centre of the battlefield, where the main concentrations have been recovered. The absence of finds from the northernmost survey area may simply be because it remains wholly under ridge and furrow and hence has not been ploughed since 1757 or 1792. In such situations it appears that bullets all tend to gravitate to the bottom of the plough soil and thus are very difficult to locate with a metal detector.

THE NEW SURVEY

Edgehill is the largest site on the English Battlefields Register and it is clear from contemporary accounts that the fighting spread over a wide area. There were several discrete actions behind the parliamentarian lines in addition to the main phases close to where the two armies first engaged. This makes it a challenging site to survey, difficulties compounded by the fact that the archaeology of the battle and battlefield has been extensively damaged by the construction, in the 1940s, of a major ammunition depot which was rebuilt in the 1990s with even more destructive effects in the heart of the battlefield.

The objective of the Battlefield Trust's Edgehill Survey, begun in August 2004 and running over two years, is to both reconstruct the historic terrain as it was in the mid 17th century and to recover a detailed, consistent picture of the distribution of battle related artefacts across the whole battlefield. It is hoped that this combination of data will enable the primary sources for the battle to be reinterpreted to place the initial deployments more accurately within the reconstructed terrain. It may also yield a new hypothesis as to the course of the action, developed from the well-known primary accounts but viewed in the context of the newly revealed terrain of 1642. This interpretation can then be tested with the evidence produced by the systematic survey of the battle archaeology. This approach is part of a programme of wider research to develop a methodology for systematic investigation of battlefields that can be applied across the UK, to achieve a degree of consistency and comparability between investigations of different battlefields. Because of the dependence in Britain upon amateur metal detecting in achieving almost all battlefield survey, the metal detecting programme aims to produce a simplified but effective fieldwork method which, because it exploits relatively standard new technology and uses basic survey methods, can be easily and cheaply applied by individuals as well as survey teams with the minimum of professional archaeological support.

THE HISTORIC TERRAIN

All the historic maps for the parishes of Kineton and Radway, together with relevant maps from all the other parishes that impinge upon or abut the battlefield, are being examined. Relevant data is then accurately transcribed onto a 1:10560 scale Ordnance Survey map base of the 1880s in a computer based mapping system, using a method previously described in a study of the Sedgemoor battlefield.[9] Where maps have not survived, particularly for Great and Little Kineton, then the Enclosure Awards are being used to reconstruct the extent of ancient enclosure and of open field strip cultivation in the 18th century, immediately prior to enclosure. To date this work has only reconstructed the pattern of open field, hedges and ancient enclosures in the century or so following the battle. When this initial stage of mapping is completed then earlier written documents will be searched in an attempt to demonstrate which of these hedges and enclosures already existed in 1642. What is already certain is that land which was still open field in the 18th century will have been open in 1642. The other important element of the landscape reconstruction is coming from the archaeology. Edgehill has by far the best earthwork evidence of any English

Figure 4: The earthwork remains of the strip field system has been destroyed over much of the battlefield during the last 50 years, but it still survives in some peripheral areas, as here on the slopes overlooking the battlefield.

battlefield for the strip field system, which was still functioning across most of the battlefield in the mid 17th century. Though over most of the battlefield these earthworks have been destroyed by ploughing in the last 50 years, they are preserved in dramatic detail on the RAF vertical air photos of 1947. Computerised mapping of this data will provide the detail not only of the strip fields but also of any small areas of unploughed meadow or pasture, typically alongside the small streams. In many cases it also reveals the course of the streams before they were straightened and deepened, in the 18th century or later, to improve drainage of the local, sticky clay soils which still become waterlogged in winter.

The interim results of this mapping show that the land of Great and Little Kineton and of Radway remained largely under open field at the time of the battle. However by the early to mid 18th century, and almost certainly already in the mid 17th century, most of the surrounding areas in adjacent parishes abutting these open fields had already been enclosed in hedged fields and converted to pasture. In addition, and of great significance in the decisions taken by Essex in deploying his forces, there appears to have been a long hedge and an area of small enclosures along more than half of the parish boundary between Kineton and Radway. While the vast majority of the open fields will have been under arable crops as the ridge and furrow demonstrates almost all of this land had been in the medieval period, it is possible that limited areas had been put down to grass by 1642. A small extent may even have had furze bushes, as one of the battle accounts suggests. However we have not yet conducted the detailed study of the written documents that might reveal the presence and exact location of such pasture and furze, or indeed of other isolated hedges within Kineton open fields.

It would seem that the choice of battlefield was determined, in part at least, by the potential to exploit cavalry in this open landscape. The exact location of the parliamentarian deployment was probably determined by Essex's wish to anchor his flanks on the enclosures to north east and south west, to make it difficult for the royalists to outflank him. The long hedge is almost certainly that which Essex lined with musketeers to provide cover in front of his left wing of cavalry. Although most contour mapping available for the battlefield is too coarse to reveal the fine detail of topography, there are very clear if slight slopes in the centre of the field which will have provided important dead ground in which Essex could deploy his infantry, out of view from the royalist lines and protected from their cannon fire. On the left however the rising ground lay just behind the long hedge, which Essex lined with musketeers, and it is likely that the artillery he deployed on this wing was placed on this higher ground. His cavalry, interlined with musketeers, could also have been positioned here. On this rise the cavalry would have been sufficiently far back from the hedge to be able to meet the enemy at a charge, if and when the latter cleared the long hedge. On the parliament right however the ground is more level, only rising northwestward towards Graveyard Coppice and the Oaks. Here the long hedge may have stopped, leaving a wholly open area that gave Essex's men no particular protection until the enclosures were reached on the far right, in the parish of Tysoe. Though Young shows Essex's right wing deployed up on the heights of The Oaks, this seems much too far back. Instead he must surely have exploited the hedged enclosures of Tysoe to anchor his right flank, placing his musketeers and dragoons along these hedge lines. The analysis of the fine detail of the terrain of the battlefield,

Figure 5: Only a handful of hedgerows in the heart of the battlefield existed in 1642. This is probably one of them, the reverse 'S' alignment reflecting the fact that it was laid out along the furrow of an open field strip. Here we are looking along the line of the royalist initial advance from the stream towards the parliamentarian infantry deployment, which was along the top of the slope. Bullets, some of them incoming fire from the parliamentarian musketeers at the beginning of the battle, lie all across this gently sloping ground.

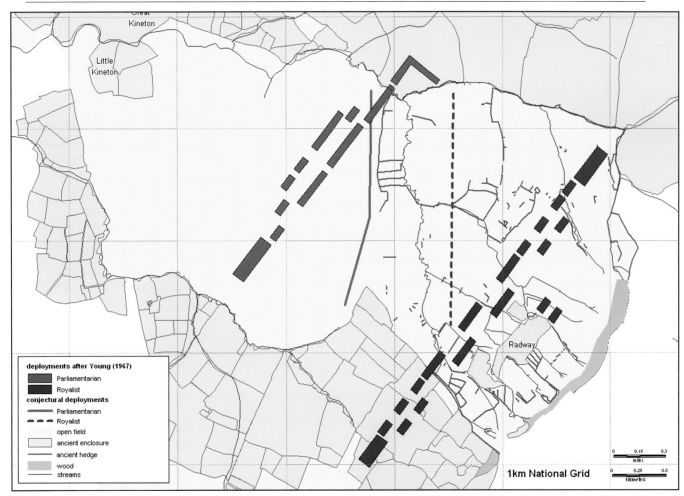

Figure 6: An interim plan of the historic terrain, also showing Young's suggested deployments together with the alternative first proposed by Pannet on the evidence of the ancient enclosures.

in association with the historic mapping, is being facilitated by Getmapping, who have donated a copy of the relevant area of their new 5-metre UK digital terrain model for the use of the Edgehill survey. So a much more sophisticated analysis than that presented here should soon be possible.

SURVEYING THE BATTLE ARCHAEOLOGY

To date in the UK all surveys of the battle archaeology of whole battlefields have been undertaken by one or two individuals over a decade or more, attempting to recover 'all' the artefacts by intensive survey. This is not a practical approach to the study of battlefields nationally. What is required is a sampling methodology which enables more rapid and consistent recovery of broad patterning, to establish the extent of the action, followed up by more intensive sampling in specific areas to reveal the detail of elements of the action. The Edgehill survey is initially using 10m spaced transects across the accessible area in an attempt to recover a consistent picture of the distribution of battle artefacts,

mainly lead bullets, across the whole battlefield. 'Hand held' GPS units, the type of satellite navigation equipment typically used by fell walkers, are being used for recording purposes in the survey. Each detectorist originally carried a GPS unit on their belts or on a lanyard, but it was found that occasionally their body would shield the GPS and cause a loss of signal, so now they are attached to each metal detector with plastic cable ties. GPS is being used to record both individual find locations and to collect 'track' information every 15 seconds, to record the exact location and intensity of survey by each detectorist. A second stage of work will later re-examine sample fields, again at 10m intervals, to determine how consistent the results are with the 10m transect survey under different conditions and in different years. Finally there will be more intensive survey work, covering all the surface area of particular fields, to again test the consistency of the battlefield wide survey and hopefully to provide a much larger sample of bullets for study.

Work began across the core of the battlefield, in the

49

Figure 7: Since August 2004 a team of six or seven metal detectorists have been out almost every Sunday systematically searching the battlefield.

area where terrain and documentary evidence suggested the two armies initially deployed. After covering most of the frontage we are now working back in either direction until the distribution of bullets fades out. The most basic of survey methods are used to lay out the transects. Four ranging poles, one with right angle sighting slots, are used to lay out two parallel baselines close to either end of the field. A 100m tape is then used to measure along the baselines for laying out of the 10m spaced transects. These are marked on the baselines with 4ft long canes, prepared with coloured flags, rotating between two colours from one transect to the next and with a third colour to mark the 6th or 7th transect, depending on how many detectorists are working that day. A minimum of 2 other similarly coloured flags are positioned by eye at the field edge at either end of each transect. These allow the detectorist always to be able to check the accuracy of his path along the transect by sighting along the flags. In this way a fairly consistent sample of about 15% of the surface area of the field is detected, distributed evenly across the field in parallel transects. Whether 15% coverage proves adequate to recover a representative sample of the artefacts has yet to be established. However, with such an extensive area to survey it was felt to be the most sensible sampling level at which to start if the whole battlefield was to be covered in the survey period.

Recording of find locations is using GPS, which generally claims an accuracy of better than ±5m, except where view of the sky is obscured, usually only

experienced at Edgehill when within about 10m of a dense belt of woodland. The one problem with the GPS has been the additional error added by the algorithms which most types of software use to convert the satellite data to the National Grid coordinates and an error correction has to be added to resolve this.[10] Every find is dug by the detectorist immediately it is located and is put into a separate bag which is marked with the finder's initials and the GPS waypoint number. This enables the exact location of each artefact to be mapped once the data has been downloaded from the GPS into the computer mapping software.

All detecting is being undertaken in discrimination mode to exclude iron, as far as practicable, without discarding signals for smaller non-ferrous artefacts such as pistol balls. All previous surveys of battle archaeology on Civil War sites have recovered a very small percentage of ferrous objects. The vast majority of finds are always lead bullets. As the initial objective of the present survey is to recover, as rapidly as possible, an overall pattern representing the distribution of action across the whole battlefield, so it is appropriate to focus primarily on lead bullets. The vast number of ferrous artefacts, mainly of post battle date, present on the field would render

Figure 8: 'Garmin etrex Venture' GPS units, now costing well under £150 each, with their essential protective cases, are attached to each of the metal detectors. They are used to record the 'waypoint' location of every find and to record the track followed by the detectorist. The data is then downloaded using 'GPS Utility' software and imported into 'MapInfo' GIS for mapping and analysis.

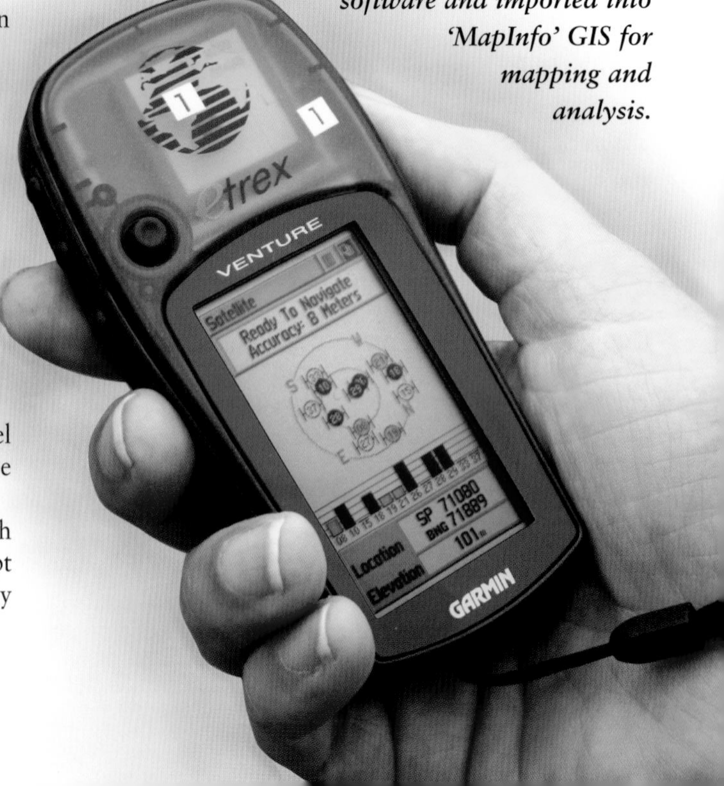

Figure 9: Lead bullets of varying calibre, fired in their tens of thousands during the battle, are the main archaeological evidence for the action.

Figure 10: The pewter top with spout, from the priming flask of a musketeer's bandolier.

Figure 11: This mid 17th century coin, found on the battlefield, might have been lost during the action, but could just as easily have been deposited on the fields along with manure from the middens in Kineton village.

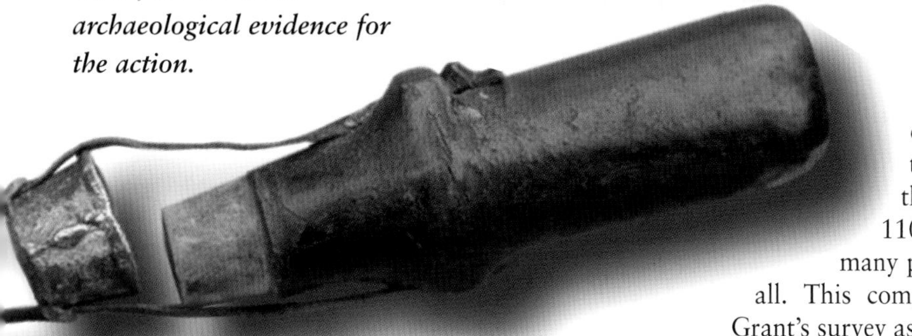

Figure 12: An example of an original 17th century powder box with a pewter cap (said to have been discovered in a house in York). If lost during the action the leather covered wooden box would have decayed in the ground, but the pewter cap will have survived. A number of these caps have been found during the survey.

extensive 'all metal' detecting impractical. It is however intended in 2005-6 to return to selected areas with the densest bullet distributions but where there is the lowest density of later debris, to conduct intensive survey in all metal mode. This should show whether a significant number of battle related ferrous artefacts can be recovered from the area of most intense infantry action. If positive results are achieved in the sample areas then further all metal sampling will be considered.

By February 2005 the survey had covered some 1.7 square kilometres and recovered over 200 bullets, with a recovery rate of about 120 minutes per ball. When calculated by hectare it can be seen that this varies from 16 minutes per bullet in the areas of most intensive action to over 110 minutes in the least dense areas, with many peripheral areas producing no bullets at all. This compares to 121 minutes per bullet for Grant's survey as a whole and 21 minutes per ball in the densest area. Almost all the certainly battle related artefacts recovered are lead bullets. These projectiles fall into three main classes: lead ball, lead slug (seven items) and what appear to be lead case shot (eleven items, of which several are musket calibre ball and the rest irregular pieces of lead). In addition there are 6 pewter caps from powder boxes and one priming flask top, all from musketeers' bandoliers. There are also four possible lead wrappers, which were used to hold a flint protectively in the jaws of the lock of a flintlock musket. In addition there are various coins and other artefacts of the 17th century, such as buckles and buttons, which may relate to the battle. However these other items could just as easily have been domestic in origin, deposited with the manure carried out to the fields in the mid 17th century from the village middens, for a large part of the battlefield was probably still under arable cultivation in the 1640s.

Each bullet is being weighed to an accuracy of around ± 0.05 gram with electronic scales and its maximum and minimum dimensions measured with electronic callipers. Even where a bullet has been distorted by an impact, the

51

original calibre can be calculated from its weight. They range in calibre from 11 bore to 45 bore (the few lesser items are quarter balls or other oddities). There is a high concentration on 12 bore, but with distinct groupings apparently relating to pistol and carbine as well as musket. These bullets are also being analysed for detail of manufacture (sprew, sprew snip and mould line or 'flash'), whether they have been fired (for which a range of distinctive attributes are present to greater or lesser degree on a large proportion of the balls) and whether they were impacted. In addition there are a small number showing evidence of having been bitten or heavily chewed. Discussion of the results of this more detailed analysis must however await recovery of far larger numbers of bullets.

Figure 13: The typical equipment of a musketeer of the 1640s, armed with a matchlock musket and a sword. From his bandolier hang wooden powder boxes, in this case with pewter tops though many will have been wholly of wood. Each box contained a single charge of gunpowder. The priming flask hangs beneath the bullet bag on his right side.

Assuming a windage of circa 1.5 - 2mm, we can interpret the calibre of the Edgehill bullets by reference to the bore of the Littlecote collection of surviving 17th century firearms, now in the Royal Armouries. Although close inspection of the Littlecote collection and various documentary sources makes clear that a simple association between calibre, weapon type and type of troops cannot always be assumed, some general conclusions can be drawn. Pistols will probably rarely be above 28 bore, though Blackmore quotes records of 1670 and 1630 giving 24 bore pistols.[11] The carbine (580 - 800 mm length) ranges in calibre from 26 - 19 bore. The muskets (above 914mm length) include a few weapons between 26 - 17 bore, more 16-13 bore and with the vast majority being 12 bore. There are just a handful of 11 bore and above, representing what have been suggested as blunderbuss or dragons, at 11 - 10 bore. The Edgehill data, as seen in the graph, fits reasonably well with these three major groupings of musket, carbine and pistol.

INITIAL CONCLUSIONS

We have already seen that the reconstruction of the historic terrain suggests a need for revision in the location and width of frontage of the two armies. The battle archaeology can be seen to provide strong supporting evidence for this reinterpretation, once one takes into account the gaps in the pattern, caused mainly by the destruction resulting from construction from the 1940s onwards of silos and railways of the MOD

Figure 14: This graph of the proportion of bullets of each calibre shows three distinct groupings which broadly correspond to pistols, carbines and muskets.

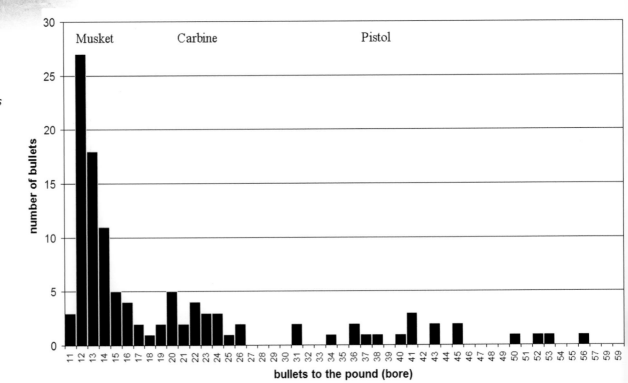

Calibre of bullets

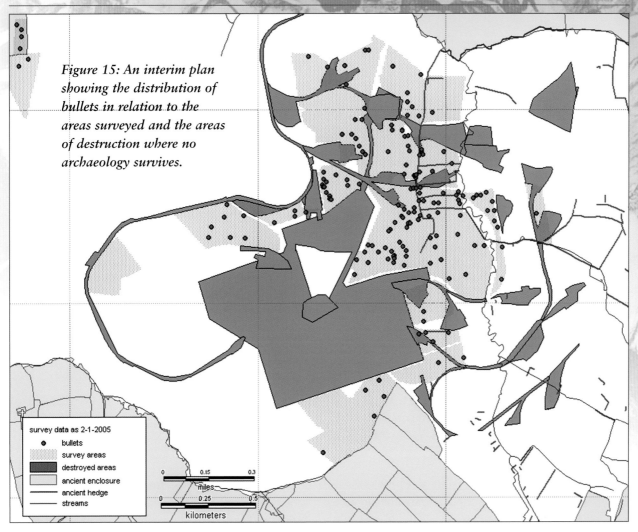

Figure 15: An interim plan showing the distribution of bullets in relation to the areas surveyed and the areas of destruction where no archaeology survives.

survey data as 2-1-2005
- bullets
- survey areas
- destroyed areas
- ancient enclosure
- ancient hedge
- streams

0   0.15   0.3
miles

0   0.25   0.5
kilometers

munitions depot. A more intense central distribution of bullets represents the infantry engagement. To the north there is a fall off in the number of bullets as one moves into the cavalry action, but there are still bullets here which might relate to the action of the musketeers on this flank. Towards the southern end of the frontage any such division is obscured by the extensive destruction caused by the modern depot, although by the time one gets to the south of the depot the density is very low, again suggesting that here, in close proximity to the enclosures of Tysoe, we are into the cavalry action once more. Within the depot most of Graveyard Coppice does survive undisturbed and it is hoped that it may be possible at some time during the survey to examine this area, as the one remaining sample of the very core of the infantry action. The action against the baggage train may be represented by the bullets recovered on the edge of the ancient enclosures of Little Kineton, on the northwestern edge of the map. Although we have so far only examined two small fields in this area, the Two Men in a Trench team recovered more bullets further to the northwest, within the enclosures. It is our intention to explore all these pasture fields later during the survey if possible.

It is in the centre of the field that the greatest potential may exist for the interpretation of the detail of the action from the bullets and other military artefacts. Although we have too few bullets at present, there are initial clues. For example, two groups of case shot may suggest the location of artillery pieces. The density of the bullets tails off to the west, suggesting we may have found the western edge of the infantry action, indicating that it was indeed in the area of Graveyard Coppice or just to its west that the parliamentarians held the royalist infantry advance. To the east of the long hedge intense distributions of bullets on the east side of the stream, not yet added to our maps, may identify the location of the intense fire-fight with which the battle ended in the autumn twilight, with the stream being the ditch referred to in the contemporary accounts. However other as yet unmapped bullets lie in a rather isolated grouping in the area of hedgerows further east and these may in fact eventually prove to be the location of this last phase of the battle.

What we have described here is just a taster of what is to come. The evidence is suggestive of various new interpretations of the location, character and intensity of the action, but far more evidence needs to be collected.

This is an exciting project in which to be involved. There is the anticipation of a story being revealed before your eyes as the hedges and the bullets progressively appear on the computer screen. There is the satisfaction every time you find another bullet to add to the pattern, not to mention the friendly competition between everyone in the detecting team to see who finds the first or the most bullets, silver coin or other notable artefact on a particular day. Everyone involved in the survey, whether looking at maps and documents, antiquarian reports, air photos, scanning artefacts, counting hedgerow species or collecting bullets - each have their own perspective on the survey and each get their own particular satisfaction from the work they are doing. All play a valuable part in an important new study. But, over the coming months, when you look out of the window on a cold, wet or windy Sunday morning, give a thought to the small but dedicated team of metal detectorists out there at Edgehill, looking for the most tangible and evocative evidence of one of our most important historic battles, a history that in at least a small way their work is beginning to rewrite.

ACKNOWLEDGEMENTS

The survey is largely the work of a team of volunteers. The following have all participated in the project and without them the work would not be possible: Derek Batten, David Beaumont, Elizabeth Beaumont, Tracey Britnell, Simon Bromet, Rosalind Burgess, Peter Burton, Jan Freeman, David Freke, Bryn Gethin, Joanna Kendal, Clive Kibblewhite, Bob Kings, John Kliene, Charles Macpharlane, Lee Macpharlane, Peter Marren, Simon Marsh, Jennifer Meir, Josie Neal, Brian Pollard, Ray Simpson, Mark Webb, Richard Young. Thanks are also due to Lt. Col. Ingle and others at DM Kineton who have facilitated access to the greater part of the site; the various other landowners who are kindly giving us access to their land; Angie Bolton, Finds Liaison Officer for Warwickshire for her work on the artefacts; other staff of the County Museums Service for their assistance and support; and staff of the Royal Armouries for specialist advice on the military finds. The Battlefields Trust is also grateful for the grant provided towards the costs of the survey by the Local Heritage Initiative. All photographs are by David Beaumont and Glenn Foard; digital mapping by Tracey Britnell; particular mention should also be made of Bob Kings, who played a key role in establishing the practical survey methods and in training the inexperienced detectorists in the team.

BIBLIOGRAPHY

Ainsworth, Stuart, and Bernard Thomason. *Where on earth are we? : the Global Positioning System (GPS) in archaeological field survey.* Swindon: English Heritage, 2003.

Blackmore, David. *Arms and Armour of the English Civil Wars.* London: Royal Armouries, 1990.

Burne, Alfred Higgins. *The Battlefields of England.* London: Methuen & Co., 1950.

English Heritage. *Battlefield Report: Edgehill 1642.* 1994.

Foard, Glenn. *The Archaeology of Attack: battles and sieges of the English Civil War. In Fields of conflict: progress and prospect in battlefield archaeology,* edited by Freeman, 87-103, 2001.

English Battlefields 991 - 1685: A Review of Problems and Potentials. Edited by Douglas D Scott, M. Haecker Charles and Larry Babbits, *Fields of Conflict III.* Nashville, forthcoming.

Naseby: The Decisive Campaign. Whitstable: Pryor Publications, 1995.

"*Sedgemoor 1685: Historic Terrain, the 'Archaeology of Battles' and the revision of Military History.*" Landscapes 4, no. 2 (2003): 5-15.

Roberts, Keith and John Tincey. *Edgehill 1642.* Oxford: Osprey, 2001.

Scott, Christopher L, Alan Turton and E. E. Gruber von Arni. *Edgehill: The Battle Reinterpreted.* Barnsley: Pen & Sword, 2004.

Tennant, Philip. *Edgehill and beyond : the people's war in the South Midlands 1642-1645.* Stroud: Alan Sutton, 1992.

Young, Peter. *Edgehill 1642: the campaign and the battle.* Kineton: Roundwood Press, 1967.

[1] English Heritage, 1994, Young (1967) and Tennant, (1992)

[2] A detailed bibliography is provided in Scott et al (2004)

[3] Roberts and Tincey, (2001), Scott et al

[4] Burne, (1950)

[5] Young, (1967)

[6] Pannet's unpublished plan is in the Edgehill Registered Battlefield file held by English Heritage

[7] Foard, (1995)

[8] An overview of potential is provided in Foard, forthcoming

[9] Foard, (2003)

[10] The problems and solutions are discussed in Ainsworth and Thomason, (2003)

[11] Data on the bore of the weapons in the Littlecote Collection was obtained from the catalogue in the Royal Armouries. Blackmore, (1990).

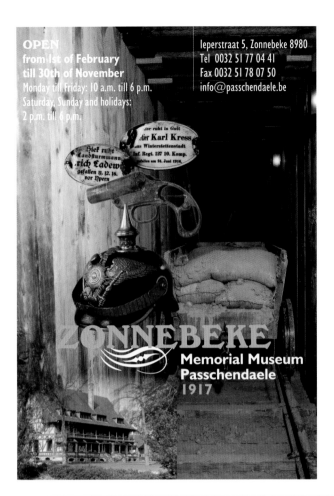

"The Ministry of War has bought about 30 acres in the local district. The site will be used for putting up a fort of the fortress of Mainz."

An article in the Ingelheimer Anzeiger - 1908

THE AERIAL ARCHAEOLOGY OF MILITARY SITES IN THE REGION OF MAINZ, RHINELAND-PALATINATE IN GERMANY

Traces left behind by a battle cannot be concealed and committed observers will spot them in the form of archaeological finds. But what if one finds scars of military activity in places where no battle, as such, was ever fought? Such locations, in conjunction with finds of military equipment, are certainly indications of military activity and can be manifestations of specific conflicts - conflicts which did not necessarily involve fighting at those sites. Dr Peter Haupt, specialist in archaeological prospection at the Johannes Gutenberg University in Mainz, examines some cases to be found in the area surrounding Mainz in the Rhineland-Palatinate.

By Dr Peter Haupt

A S A CITY LOCATED ON THE RIVER RHINE – an enduring political border – Mainz was in the theatre of war for many armed conflicts during the past 2,000 years. Such activities took place at an ever-increasing distance from the city because of the developing science of fortification. Since the 17th century fortifications such as temporary entrenchments and approach trenches have been situated in agricultural areas and are therefore accessible to aerial archaeology techniques.

The battles within the period of the First Coalition War at the end of the 18th century are particularly significant. From May to July 1793 different German armies laid siege to the French forces occupying Mainz, which capitulated quickly. In 1794 and 1795 French forces in their turn besieged the town, which was finally awarded to France in the Peace of Campo Formio in 1797. Only aerial archaeology is able to supply interpretation in this case which cannot be gained from contemporary plans and maps.

An aerial photograph taken in 1999 indicates a strange, angled trench north of the village of Ober-Olm (figure 1). This trench can be identified as a rear line bulwark of the French siege from 1794/95 according to a copperplate engraving - Inv. No. GS 1991/205- in the regional museum of Mainz, yet there has never been any fighting there. On the copperplate engraving of course, the units are merely represented as tactical symbols; that they did not simply pitch their tents but also entrenched

Figure 1- Fortification of 1794/95, visible from crop marks. P HAUPT, JULY 1999

Figure 2 - Fortification (trenches) of the mid 1790s. P HAUPT, JULY 1994

the hills surrounding Mainz during the two sieges of the mid - 1790s. Surveys, during which a good deal of modern pottery, a Prussian military button, and other military objects were discovered, hint at the presence of armed forces for an extended period. Despite the finds mentioned above no fighting is recorded as having taken place at this location; the objects could simply have been lost during the course of daily life – a pot smashed here, a button torn off there - without any fighting actually taking place.

THE FORT WAS ON THE RIDGE ALONG THE RIVER

The trenches of a fort above the village of Bodenheim, about 8 kilometres south of Mainz, are a little older (Figures 3 & 4). The fort was on the ridge along the river Rhine, directed at Mainz, and dates back to the 17th c. on account of its shape. It is almost square in layout and three sides are fortified. The fourth side is furthest away from any enemy force and thus there was not the necessity to reinforce it to the same extent as the other three sides. Surveys here did not result in obvious finds which could provide evidence of the site's history. There could be a connection with a siege of the Thirty Years' War but the fort could just as well have been built some decades later within the scope of the French activity during the War of the Palatinate Succession.

there can be ascertained from the aerial photograph. Over time this trench was infilled. Archaeologists can deduce this by examining the planted grain: it thrives because of the better water retention properties of the loose and thoroughly mixed soil of the entrenchment, which enables the plants to grow for a longer period and thus makes them stand out from the surrounding grain which has already ripened.

By the same token an entrenchment between the suburbs of Drais and Marienborn is visible on the second photograph (Figure 2). This was one of the trenches which formed the ring of the besieging forces on

Figures 3 and 4 - Fort of the 17th century. P HAUPT, JULY 1994

3

4

The old fortifications of Mainz itself, limited the town in the 19th century to an area from the citadel to the Kästrich and towards the modern part of today's town. Due to the use of new weapons, including the invention of the highly explosive grenade around 1885, these 17th century defences clearly became obsolete. Fortifications had thus to be strengthened with concrete and iron if they were to stand any chance of resisting enemy bombardment.

At the turn of the 19th century different strategies led to a reduction of the ramparts in the case of most forts. Instead a framework of fortified constructions was built on the rise to the west and south of the town. In case of war this network could be utilised to form an armed bridgehead on the left bank of the river Rhine. In addition, the town could also expand in its old ring of fortifications. From 1909 to 1912 the municipal

hospitals were built in the area of the Kästrich. The replacement of the old fortifications stretched over the plateau east of the Selz valley and the nearby villages of Harxheim, Gau-Bischofsheim, Bodenheim, and Laubenheim; a distance of 5-12 kilometres south and west of the old defences (see map Figure 5).

Work began in 1908, in peacetime, and first to be completed was the main part of the ring defence. An article in the Ingelheimer Anzeiger of 24th September 1908 observed that,

> "*In der hiesigen Gemarkung hat der Militärfiskus etwa 30 Morgen Ackerland gekauft. Das Gelände wird zum Bau eines Forts der Festung Mainz verwendet.*" ("The Ministry of War has bought about 30 acres in the local district. The site will be used for putting up a fort of the fortress of Mainz.") [1]

Figure 5 - Map of the recognized archaeological traces of fortifications in the Mainz area. MAPPED BY THE AUTHOR,

GEOBASISINFORMATIONEN (TK50) © LANDESAMT FÜR VERMESSUNG UND GEOBASISINFORMATIONEN RHEINLAND-PFALZ VOM 09.02.2005, AZ.: 26 722-1.401

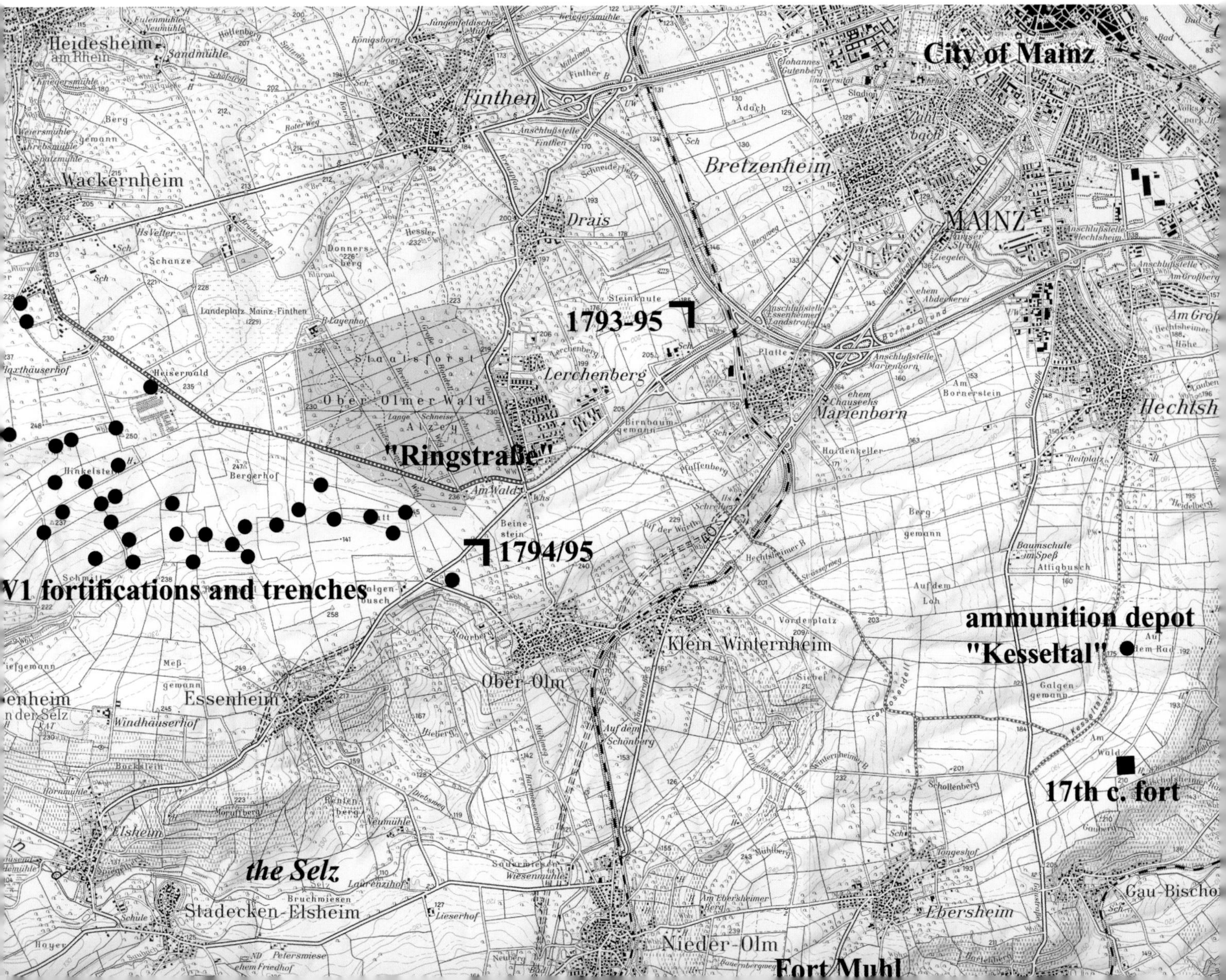

First of all, a supply route was built (the so called 'Ringstraße' with a width of 3.50m) in the immediate vicinity of the front line. Even today this route passes along the 'Rabenkopf' at Wackernheim to the forest of Ober-Olm and from there onwards via Lerchenberg to Ebersheim. It is still in use as an agricultural track today. At the 'Franzosendell' (Frenchmen's Hollow; a field name which recalls the siege of 1794/5) the road branches; one branch leading to Ebersheim and therefore to the outer positions as well as to Fort Muhl south of the village, the second closing the ring by including the Hechtsheimer Kesseltal.

Fortification railways (with a gauge of 0.6 - 1.0 m) were built in 1909 and 1913. They partially followed the ring road as a 'ring line'; their main function, however, was to connect the newly built fortifications and the stations of Mainz to ensure the flow of supplies. Water pipes were put down in two stages in 1908/09 and 1912/13. Additionally, two water tanks were erected in 1908; one at the edge of the Ober-Olm forest - capacity 81.10m - and another in 1912 around 1.5 kilometres south-east of the Haxthäuser Hof with a possible capacity of 155m. In the aerial photograph this armoured water tank can be seen as a small clump of trees (Figure 6). The water pipes, noticeable as crop marks, are interesting too, especially those which can be seen crossing a sugar-beet field as a dark line at the lower edge of the picture.

Also in 1908, telegraph lines were dug in to a depth of at least 1.25m to protect them from sabotage and shelling. The telephone network was extended in 1914.

Figure 6 - Armoured water tank (clump of trees) with water pipes (built 1912). P HAUPT, JULY 1996

In 1909 six telegraph exchanges were constructed as concrete command posts. A seventh telegraph exchange at the 'Rabenkopf' followed connected to an ammunition store in 1910. At the same time two additional ammunition stores were finished at Wackernheim and Ebersheim.

An infantry fort called 'Auf der Muhl' was built southeast of Ebersheim between 1909 and 1911. It was a strong, concreted fortress for a garrison of 300 men.

During the few remaining years of peace all buildings were made secure. In the summer of 1913 a manoeuvre involving a fortress-detachment of airshipmen took place close to the position of Ober-Ingelheim.

With the onset of the First World War in August 1914 the reinforcement of the positions continued and went on until 1915. According to research by F. Fischer the following concrete buildings were put up:

59 infantry shelters (I-rooms)
55 guardrooms and 148 dug-outs
28 artillery shelters (A-rooms)
17 ammunition stores (M-rooms)
9 artillery observation posts
1 machine gun position
and 1 water tank (near Gau-Bischofsheim) [2]

Thus, 318 concrete buildings were added to the ten structures which had already existed from earlier periods. 13 infantry battalions (without reserves) would have been the garrison force of these positions which were meant to serve as a bridgehead in case of an allied breakthrough on the Western Front. These concrete constructions were connected by zigzag communication-trenches, which, in turn, led to the trenches of the front-line (Figure 7-9).

An ammunition depot at the Kesseltal near Hechtsheim which can be observed in the crop marks (Figure 10) is especially interesting: the track, as well as the actual underground depot, is clearly visible – although the position itself is exploited agriculturally.

Figure 7 and 8 - Opposite left to right: trenches of 1914/15. P HAUPT, JUNE 1997

Figure 9 - Artillery shelter of 1914/15 with traces of water pipes or telegraph lines. P HAUPT, JULY 1994

Figure 10 - Ammunition depot of 1914/15. P HAUPT, JULY 1993

It was article 180 of the Treaty of Versailles that determined the fate of the fortified positions around Mainz:

> 'All fortified works, fortresses and field works situated in German territory to the west of a line drawn fifty kilometres to the east of the Rhine shall be disarmed and dismantled.'

The entire construction had to be dismantled. Considering the severe supply problems faced by Germany at that time a great deal of arable land reverted to agricultural production. Water pipelines were kept in part to supply civil buildings such as the Haxthäuser Hof or the Layenhof. However, the water tank on the Gauberg hill next to Gau-Bischofsheim, as well as the water pipes serving the fortified positions were demolished and dismantled, as was every telegraph and telephone line.

At the beginning of 1922 the demolition conducted by the French General Nollet under the auspices of the Interallied Military Control Commission, had been completed.[3] This commission had also controlled the dismantling of the fortress of Mainz in line with the compulsory disarmament of the German Reich. This was why all shelters were blown up in 1921 but six years later positions were still being dismantled as the newspaper of Ingelheim reported on 26th March 1927:

> *"Ingelheim. Z.Z. werden die im Herbst 1914 unnötigerweise gebauten Feldbefestigungen, die in Dutzenden auf den Höhen der Gemarkung Nieder-Ingelheim, Heidesheim und Wackernheim erbaut worden sind, gesprengt."* ("Ingelheim. At the moment all field positions that were not needed and erected by the dozen on the hills of the landmark of Nieder-Ingelheim, Heidesheim, and Wackernheim are now blown up.")[4]

The resulting rubble from the destruction of the concrete buildings was partially collected within the larger dugout ruins. Today, those ruins stand out clearly as small thickets, although they are incompletely marked as small hills with artificial escarpments on topographic maps. Communication trenches and ditches in open country were filled in.

Likewise, Fort Muhl, the most solid building of the fortified ring, was blown up in 1921 although its trenches remained open. Unfortunately, they are increasingly levelled today because of agricultural use and as a result of earth deposition. Buildings above ground which are – except for the streets and tracks – limited to dug-out ruins, have been mapped with the help of surveys, aerial photographs, and topographic maps. Apart from modern images one aerial photograph taken by Hansa Luftbild GmbH in April 1934 is especially worth mentioning as it shows many of the shelters that were blown up, and that in spite of its small scale of 1:25.000.

Levelled communication trenches and ditches, smaller and incompletely excavated concrete shelters, telegraph and telephone lines and other interventions in the earth, are not recognisable in relief for the most part. But they are all within the scope of the work of the aerial archaeologist. First, the levelled trenches and dug-outs can be recognised clearly as crop marks. In June particularly the grain, and sometimes sugar beet, grows much better on levelled ground than on the uneven ground of the surrounding fields. Corresponding soil marks are revealed from the discolouration of the earth's surface by regrouping or accumulations with organic substances. Such marks cannot be spotted in winter.

In the same way we are missing spectacular architectural finds like the tower which was built on the Petersaue pasture in the Rhine between Mainz and Mainz-Amöneburg. This tower was part of the fortress as well. Missing such finds depends on the different nature of the ground on the one hand as gravelled areas from rivers are more susceptible to drying out and therefore to show crop marks. On the other hand one can begin to understand a different concept of fortress: large positions above ground would have meant a large 'footprint' and therefore would present a large target for any enemy bombardment. That is why the 20th century positions were built from small dug-outs that only rose a little above the ground and are also scattered irregularly over a wide area. [5]

A schematic plan of the 'Entfestigungsamt' (Office for the Dismantlement of Fortifications) of Mainz from December 1920 is indispensable for interpreting the mapped findings. Important concrete buildings (shelters, ammunition stores and telegraph exchanges) as well as the ring road and the fortification railway, are marked here with numbers and an abbreviation as to their purpose. Many of the structures that were not concreted, however, (dug-outs, communications trenches, etc.) are not plotted. A textbook on camouflage against aerial reconnaissance from World War I also assists in interpreting the aerial photographs.[6] Here, one can study examples of relatively better or worse camouflaged positions of varying kinds. Contemporary documents like photographs and the collection of pictures and maps at the municipal archive of Mainz are also worth mentioning. Contemporary aerial photographs of the position are not to hand at the current time (inquiries for aerial photographs of the area around Mainz during World War I and the 1920s made to the Service Historique, armée de terre, Vincennes, France, the Air Photo Library, University of Keele, the RAF Museum, London and The National Archives in London, have so far met with little success.)

Mainz was repeatedly affected by bombardment during the course of the war, which caused considerable damage and led to a number of lives being lost. It might be reasonable to expect therefore, that the fortified positions had been documented by allied aerial reconnaissance.

Finally, a newspaper article of 13th March 1911 suggests that some surveys from the air may have been associated with the fortified positions years before the war's outbreak:

"*Mit Rücksicht auf die Außenbefestigungswerke von Mainz bis in unsere Gegend ist auf Antrag des Berliner Kriegsministeriums eine Polizeiverordnung erlassen worden, wonach Passagierflüge mit Flugzeugen, mit Luftschiffen und Fesselballons auch innerhalb der Gemarkung Ober-und Niederingelheim nur mit schriftlicher Erlaubnis des Gouvernements der Festung Mainz erlaubt sind.*" ("*Considering the extent of the outlying fortifications of Mainz up to our area, the Ministry of War has issued a decree whereupon passenger flights with planes, airships, and captive balloons within the landmark of Ober-and Niederingelheim are allowed only with the written permission of the government of the fortress of Mainz.*") [7]

NOTES

[1] Diehl, W. *Ingelheimer Chronik von 1899-1950* (Offenbach, 51:1974).

[2] Fischer, F. *Die Festung Mainz 1866-1921. Ein Beitrag zu ihrer Baugeschichte im Rahmen des deutschen Festungsbau* (Düsseldorf 17ff, 1970).

[3] Nollet, C.M. *Une expérience de désarmement* (Paris:1932).

[4] Diehl, W. op.cit.

[5] Ille, P. Zeitspuren. *Luftbildarchäologie in Hessen* (Wiesbaden: 84f, 1993).

[6] NN 1917: *Das taktische Lichtbilderbuch. II. Teil. Die Deckung gegen Fliegersicht* (Charleville).

[7] Diehl, W. *Ingelheimer Chronik 1899-1950* (Offenbach, 63:1974).

FURTHER READING

Students of the fortification of the area around Mainz will gain much from the detailed work undertaken by Fischer in the work *Die Festung Mainz 1866-1921. Ein Beitrag zu ihrer Baugeschichte im Rahmen des deutschen Festungsbau* (Düsseldorf 17ff: 1970).

THE GREATEST BATTLEFIELD THAT NEVER WAS: ENGLAND'S WORLD WAR II ANTI-INVASION DEFENCES AND THE NATIONAL MAPPING PROGRAMME

How great is the potential contribution of aerial survey to the study of England's military sites and landscapes? Cain Hegarty, Sarah Newsome and Helen Winton of English Heritage examine the issues surrounding this question and feature an in-depth case study of a project focused on the Suffolk coast – the greatest battlefield that never was – soon to be the subject of an English Heritage and Suffolk County Council book.

By Cain Hegarty, Sarah Newsome & Helen Winton

IN RECENT YEARS THERE HAS BEEN a growing recognition of the archaeological value of England's surviving twentieth century military remains. This, in part, is a response to the increasingly fragile condition and situation of the small proportion of sites which survive but is also a reflection of a great popular interest in the subject. A number of recent projects reflect this increased popularity, most notably the Defence of Britain project, a massive and largely volunteer run survey of the location and condition of all surviving modern military features (Defence of Britain, 2002). A comprehensive survey of documentary sources relating to the survival of many types of twentieth century military sites was also undertaken as part of English Heritage's Monument Protection Programme (Dobinson 1998).

These surveys have considered evidence from aerial photographs but an English Heritage initiative - the National Mapping Programme (NMP) - is the first national survey to use aerial photographs consistently as a main source for archaeological research in England. The programme uses aerial photographs taken during and immediately after World War II to interpret and record England's wartime defences and military installations accurately.

THE NATIONAL MAPPING PROGRAMME AND ENGLAND'S WARTIME DEFENCES

Archaeological sites have been photographed from the air since the early days of flight (Barber forthcoming). However, the real impetus for the use of aerial photographs for archaeological research was the development of military technology during World War I (Bewley 2001 75-6). Individuals such as OGS Crawford and Squadron Leader Insall pioneered the use of aerial photographs for archaeology in Britain, using their military reconnaissance skills in the years following the Great War. Crawford in particular pioneered the mapping of archaeological features from aerial photographs, enabling the analysis of past landscapes rather than individual sites. World War II saw further advances in military reconnaissance and a new generation of archaeologists, such as Derrick Riley and JKS St Joseph, drew on the technical skills gained during the war. Riley published a number of important books on landscape archaeology and St Joseph founded the Cambridge University Collection of aerial photographs.

Since the early days of aerial archaeology there have been a number of archaeological surveys using aerial photographs as a main source but these have been sporadic and tend to concentrate on recording prehistoric and Roman sub-surface features showing as cropmarks (see Wilson 1982 and 2000, Bewley 2001,

76). The National Mapping Programme is the first national project in England to apply a systematic methodology for interpreting and mapping all archaeological features, dating from the Neolithic to the early twentieth century, visible on aerial photographs. This includes recording all archaeological sites visible as cropmarks and earthworks but also structures, in particular those relating to early twentieth century military activities. For an overview of NMP see Bewley (2001).

The main sources used by NMP are the vertical and oblique aerial photographs held in the collections of the National Monuments Record (NMR) in Swindon, supplemented by collections at the University of Cambridge and the relevant Local Authority Sites and Monuments, or Historic Environment, Record. The earliest of these photographs were taken by the RAF and the USAAF in the early 1940s, on training flights to instruct aircrews in military reconnaissance techniques before they ventured into the hostile skies of World War II.

SNAPSHOTS

The major advantage of aerial photographs for the study of WWII remains is that they can provide 'snapshots' at various points in time through the 1940s. This can reveal the layout and basic structure of everything from small individual sites to whole defensive landscapes. Documentary evidence remains the core resource for the study of military remains but aerial photographs supplement these with a, sometimes unique, pictorial record of these sites, often during their peak usage, and after their removal or decline. Comparison with the documentary sources can yield interesting results where, for example, local variants of the standard military buildings arise or where the location of a structure is different from its planned site. In these cases local people who remember, or who have made particular studies of their area, are essential in understanding the remains.

NMP projects are able to look at surviving military remains from a well informed, but significantly different perspective from other projects. Archaeological surveys using 1940s aerial photographs can place the relatively few structures which remain today into the wider context of the national system of defences constructed in England in the summer of 1940, due to the increased threat after the German conquest of the Low Countries and France.

The Suffolk case study which follows will illustrate the contrast in the form of defences along this vulnerable coast compared to other parts of England.

The Suffolk coastal defences are remarkable in their continuity in contrast to other areas, such as the Norfolk coast, where the nature and geographical location of the coast means that military defences are discontinuous and large training camps are more prevalent. Away from these vulnerable areas the evidence recorded by NMP projects tends to be more varied. Cornwall NMP has recorded defensive 'landscapes' in the form of defences and wartime activity concentrated around the major ports and vulnerable areas, in particular Plymouth, and also the preparations for the D-Day landings (A. Young, E. Trevarthen pers comm). The pill boxes along organised lines of defence, such as the Taunton Stop Line or the defences along the Kennet and Avon canal, are also recorded on aerial photographs from the 1940s and, increasingly, where they survive, on more recent specialist archaeologically targeted photography taken in the last ten years. Aerial photographs also proved a major source of information for the physical remains of early twentieth century activity on the military training ranges of Salisbury Plain (McOmish, Field and Brown 2002 137- 148, Crutchley 48-50) (Figure 1).

The range and complexity of military remains visible on aerial photographs depend on the location of the NMP project area but there are site types which are typically recorded throughout England. Searchlight batteries are a common feature, either protecting particular sites, usually airfields, or as part of a network, such as the one across Lincolnshire. Aerial photographs

Figure 1 - Trenches on Salisbury Plain Training area. NMR ST 9645/13 (18659/22) 09-JAN-2000 (C) ENGLISH HERITAGE.

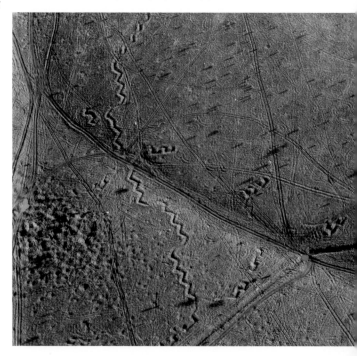

Figure 2 - An early vertical print taken to test the effectiveness of camouflage here showing Tholthorpe airfield. 78/UK705 FRAME 17, 05-NOV-1940 ENGLISH HERITAGE (NMR) RAF PHOTOGRAPHY.

Figure 3 - Prisoner of war camp in the grounds of Halswell House in Somerset. CPE/UK/1944 FRAME 2035 23-JAN-1947. ENGLISH HERITAGE (NMR) RAF PHOTOGRAPHY.

also provide a good pictorial record of the network of airfields which developed across England through both wars, but which largely declined from the 1950s onwards. Details of runways, taxi strips, ancillary buildings and supporting camps can usually be seen. Particularly interesting sites include one of Wiltshire's earliest civilian airfields, founded in 1931 but used during World War II to assemble and test Spitfires and early jet propelled aircraft (Barber, Grady and Winton 2003). Oddities include the camouflaged airfield at Tholthorpe in North Yorkshire (Figure 2) where the runways have been painted to resemble banks of trees, including features which may have been intended to appear as shadows or overhanging trees along the edges (Horne and Kershaw forthcoming).

Arguably one of the most common military sites recorded on aerial photographs from the 1940s are camps, very often situated in the grounds of large country houses. It can be difficult to positively identify the original inhabitants from the photographs alone, as the uses of the camps varied considerably and could include, for example, use as transit camps, hospitals, labour camps and prisoner of war (POW) camps. Sometimes it is possible to identify the function of a camp from distinctive features, such as a high fence and watch towers suggesting a POW camp. Many of these were hastily constructed in England towards the end of the war to cope with the influx of German captives (Figure 3).

The Suffolk coastal NMP project is an example of the successful use of aerial photographs to analyse a complex defensive landscape. As the discussion makes clear, however, aerial photographs, although essential, are only one of many resources available for studies of early twentieth century military remains. What follows is a brief overview of the Suffolk Coastal NMP project using individual sites or classes of site to illustrate a landscape of defence which, had circumstances been slightly different, could have been the focus of one of the greatest battles of World War II.

THE SUFFOLK COASTAL NMP

The Suffolk Coastal NMP project area comprised a one-kilometre strip encompassing the Suffolk coastline and a slightly wider area around the county's major estuaries, totalling 312 square kilometres. The coastal scope of the project was in part a response to the issues raised in the English Heritage/RCHME report England's Coastal Heritage (Fulford, Champion and Long, 1997), which identified the coastline as a priority area for archaeological investigation. The focus of the Suffolk mapping project was therefore on the archaeology of the coastal and inter-tidal zones, including a terrestrial 'buffer zone', to place sites located in these areas into context, and included all archaeological sites and landscapes dating from the Neolithic period to 1945.

The aerial photographs of the Suffolk coast, in particular those from the 1940s, presented the project staff with an unprecedented opportunity to interpret and record what was essentially a complete landscape of defence.

SUFFOLK'S WARTIME DEFENCES

Prior to June 1940, invasion was thought unlikely and much of the British coastline was effectively undefended. Following the Fall of France in June 1940, the threat of a German invasion and a possible Blitzkrieg 'knock-out blow' suddenly became very real. This threat was keenly felt on the East Anglian coast, a long stretch of which was identified as one of three areas most likely to be targeted by an invading landing force (Dobinson 1996b, 16). No doubt this is why, of all the Command areas, the construction of defensive works in Eastern Command, the area that included Suffolk, was the most rapid in July 1940, with 60% of defences completed within one month (Dobinson 1996b, 37).

The anti-invasion defences can be seen in such detail on some aerial photographs that, in the months immediately following June 1940, the progress of construction along the beach is discernible from month to month. As the war progressed it is clear that although the military strategy may have changed (see Dobinson 1996b), the defences themselves continued to develop and evolve into a complex and integrated system, one which inevitably greatly affected daily life on the Suffolk coast. One of the criticisms occasionally levelled against 'battlefield' archaeologists is that they are more interested in the physical remains of a conflict than in its social, cultural and political significance (Newman 2003). The political aspects are beyond the scope of the project and this piece, but the NMP project actively acknowledged the social and cultural impact of Suffolk's anti-invasion defences on the region's inhabitants and those directly involved with the defences - what could be termed the 'human' element. This aspect has been highlighted in a separate article arising from the project (Newsome 2003).

FLUID AND CHANGEABLE FRONT

By 1943 the perceived threat of invasion was lessening and some anti-invasion defences began to be dismantled while others, such as the anti-aircraft batteries, which were re-organised in late 1944 to combat the V1 flying bombs, continued to develop and change. So, although no enemy forces set foot on Suffolk's shore, and it cannot therefore be technically defined as a battlefield, the defences of the Suffolk coast formed a fluid and changeable front on which home forces actively engaged the airborne enemy, and it can therefore surely be acknowledged as a 'place of conflict' as defined by Newman (2003).

The anti-invasion defences of World War II can be roughly, if artificially, divided into two categories – passive and active, both of which were recorded by the project. The variety of form and materials is too vast to be covered here (see Lowry 1996 for a more detailed summary), but the majority of the anti-invasion beach defences that were rapidly constructed in 1940 fall within the passive category.

PASSIVE ANTI-INVASION DEFENCES

This group of defences was largely composed of linear obstructions intended to impede the progress of both the infantry and armoured vehicles of the landing forces, and most common types are illustrated in these particularly clear photographs of the beach to the north of Aldeburgh (Figure 5). An invading force, attempting to move up the beach from the sea, would first encounter a series of poles or spikes, probably intended to hole landing craft and generally only visible on the photographs when viewed stereoscopically. Then came anti-tank scaffolding, only just visible on the aerial photographs in the breaking surf, intended to force

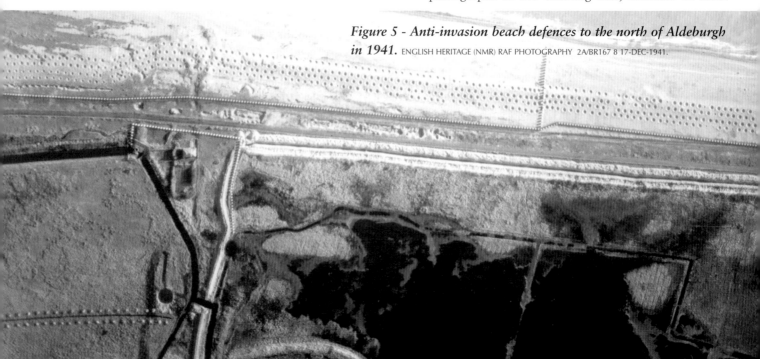

Figure 5 - Anti-invasion beach defences to the north of Aldeburgh in 1941. ENGLISH HERITAGE (NMR) RAF PHOTOGRAPHY 2A/BR167 8 17-DEC-1941.

landing tanks to reveal their vulnerable underbellies to anti-tank fire. Next, a minefield is clearly visible on these images, probably due to having been freshly laid in the shingle; once weathered the shingle would effectively hide the explosives. If the tanks survived the minefield they would once more have to risk exposing their underside if they wished to cross the line of concrete anti-tank cubes which lay behind. A deep 'v' shaped anti-tank ditch provided the final line of beach defence, very often created by widening existing drainage ditches. This was once more designed to trap any tank fortunate enough to have made it unscathed thus far. Elaborate as they were, it was not expected that these defences would stop the Germans; the best that could be expected was that they would be delayed long enough for a mobile defence force to mobilise to engage them. It is perhaps fortunate that these defences were never tested.

Barbed wire entanglements frequently formed an extra strand of the defence in depth, extensive stretches of barbed wire often defining enclosures known as 'strongpoints' which contained further defences such as slit trenches or pill boxes from which the beach could be enfiladed. Elaborate examples were constructed along extensive lengths of coastline, as can be seen here to the

south of Kessingland in 1941 (see Figure 7). The NMP survey has shown that these defences were part of a dynamic system, often evolving into more or less complex constructions over the course of the war, as the need for anti-invasion defence increased or decreased. For example, at Sizewell, two small sub-circular barbed wire defined strongpoints containing pill boxes and slit trenches can be seen on photographs taken in 1940. By 1941 the threat of invasion was perceived to be very serious and the strongpoints evolved, merging into more complex linear configurations (see Figure 6a). However, by 1944 the threat of invasion had decreased and a greater threat was posed by the V1 flying bomb. These photographs from 1945 consequently show a site which had changed its focus so much as to have been converted into an 'active' form of defence, a DIVER battery, a site-type discussed below in more detail (Figure 6b).

By the summer of 1941, such 'soft' linear defences could be traced along almost the entire coast of Suffolk, but following the end of the war much of it was almost completely removed, particularly in areas attractive to tourism. Often this left the core of 'hard' defences - pill boxes and other concrete structures - isolated and out of context, to be demolished decades later or simply left to

6a) Complex anti-invasion defences at Sizewell in 1941. RAF 2-BR167 FRAME 22 17-DEC-1941 ENGLISH HERITAGE (NMR) RAF PHOTOGRAPHY.

6b) A change of strategy: by 1945 the anti-invasion defences have been replaced by a DIVER battery.

RAF 106G-UK-929 FRAME 3203 16-OCT-1945. ENGLISH HERITAGE (NMR) RAF PHOTOGRAPHY.

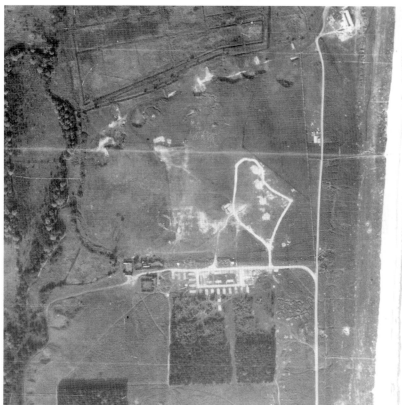

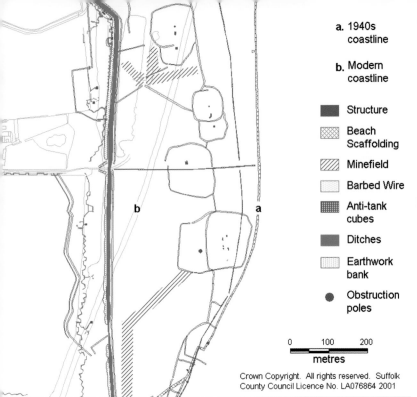

a. 1940s coastline

b. Modern coastline

▓ Structure

▨ Beach Scaffolding

▨ Minefield

▢ Barbed Wire

▦ Anti-tank cubes

▓ Ditches

▨ Earthwork bank

● Obstruction poles

0   100   200
metres

Figure 7 - Complex barbed wire defined strongpoints located on the sea front near Kessingland. Much of this landscape has since been lost to coastal erosion.

a precarious existence on the foreshore facing the ravages of the sea. For example, due to coastal erosion, one particular pillbox near the gun battery at Bawdsey now lies upside down on the beach after toppling from its original location on the cliff top, (see Newsome 2003, plate section). More drastic erosion has completely destroyed up to 300m of coast between Kessingland and Southwold, on which the entire linear anti-invasion defences for the area were located (see Figure 7). Dobinson's documentary survey did not attempt to locate these types of defences, not only because the vast numbers involved would have made the task almost impossible but also because the documentation that does exist records their location less systematically than for other types of defensive site (Dobinson, 1996b: 4). The NMP records and map representations of these defences are therefore particularly valuable in complementing other surveys by filling-in the blanks and accurately locating sites, whilst at the same time identifying key photographs which act as 'snapshots', a moment in time, recording the development of unusual forms of defence.

PASSIVE ANTI-AIRCRAFT DEFENCES

Invasion fears also included the landing of enemy forces by aircraft and anti-aircraft defences also had passive elements. The most common are known as 'anti-glider' ditches, but were in fact intended to prevent troop carriers landing in open spaces, such as fields or commons. In Suffolk they commonly take the form of a

Figure 8 - 'Anti-glider' ditches covered large swathes of coastal heath, common and marsh during the war years. Few survived the post-war agricultural expansion, an exception visible on aerial photographs is preserved at Sutton Hoo.

NMR TM2848/63 (15097/45) 28-JUN-1994 (C) ENGLISH HERITAGE. NMR

narrow ditch flanked by mounds of spoil, as can be seen on the extreme left (north) of Figure 5. These ditches covered extensive tracts of coastal heath and marsh but as with the other forms of earthwork defences, they were rapidly filled-in following the war, particularly as areas of heathland were increasingly being converted to agricultural production. A rare example can still be seen, in a much eroded form, within the area of the scheduled monument at Sutton Hoo; possibly the only scheduled 'anti-glider' ditches in the country! (see Figure 8).

ACTIVE ANTI-INVASION DEFENCES

The realisation that much of Britain's coast was effectively undefended in 1940 also prompted the construction of 'active' anti-invasion defences, which, on the Suffolk coast, consisted largely of both temporary and permanent sites, or emplacements, built to house artillery batteries. The batteries can be divided into coastal and anti-aircraft artillery.

COASTAL ARTILLERY BATTERIES

Coastal batteries were constructed to provide active protection against sea-borne forces, which may have slipped past the protection provided by the Royal Navy and RAF. As with the passive defences, the need was so urgent that many coastal batteries began life as rapidly constructed Emergency Batteries, armed with any guns available, often ex-naval stock.

One example on the sea front at Aldeburgh was first built in June 1940 as an Emergency Battery. A makeshift structure of sandbags and girders partially enclosed temporary gun platforms, which housed two naval six-inch guns of WWI vintage. A more permanent battery, built on the same site, replaced the Emergency Battery by September of the following year with concrete casemates providing protection for the gun crews. The casemates were roughly 50m apart, the northernmost gun, 'Gun 2', firing directly out to sea, with 'Gun 1' to the south

Figure 9 - Aldeburgh Coastal Battery as recorded in its wartime landscape by the National Mapping Programme.

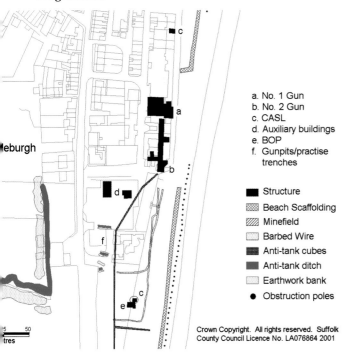

a. No. 1 Gun
b. No. 2 Gun
c. CASL
d. Auxiliary buildings
e. BOP
f. Gunpits/practise trenches

■ Structure
▧ Beach Scaffolding
▨ Minefield
▢ Barbed Wire
▦ Anti-tank cubes
■ Anti-tank ditch
▢ Earthwork bank
● Obstruction poles

angled at about 45 degrees, to provide a wider field of fire and greater cover of the beach. The battery was accompanied on the sea front by two Coastal Artillery Searchlights (CASL) and to the rear by an engine room and assorted auxiliary buildings. An old windmill on the beach was converted into a battery observation post (BOP). As can be seen in Figure 9, the battery was also surrounded by passive, coastal anti-invasion defences, and it was flanked to the north and south by strongpoints containing pillboxes, forming an integrated coastal defensive system. Unusually, elements of the Aldeburgh battery survive today; the casemate of 'Gun 1' has been converted into a beachfront shelter.

ANTI-AIRCRAFT ARTILLERY BATTERIES

It had become apparent before the war that the RAF alone would not be able to provide anti-aircraft defence for the entire country; thus anti-aircraft artillery was to play a vital role (Dobinson 2001). Heavy Anti-aircraft Artillery (HAA) batteries are relatively easy to identify on aerial photographs, the typical plan consisting of four circular or octagonal concrete and earthwork gun emplacements, most often arrayed in a semi-circular layout adjacent to, or surrounding, a central command post. Accommodation for gun crews and officers, and auxiliary buildings such as engine houses, were usually arranged along a metalled track leading to the battery. For a more detailed description of this site type see Lowry (1996).

Heavy anti-aircraft guns were in short supply initially and although most important urban centres received some anti-aircraft defence in the early 1940s, it was not until 1943 that technological developments and gun production advanced sufficiently to provide Britain with adequate and efficient anti-aircraft cover (Dobinson 2001). Indeed, on the Suffolk coast it appears that the majority of HAA batteries recorded by the NMP project date from 1944 onwards. This may reflect later wartime developments and will be discussed below.

Very few of the fifty or so HAA sites recorded by NMP on the Suffolk coast were constructed prior to mid-1944. However, a good example is visible at Lowestoft on aerial photographs of April 1944. This site shows the typical concrete and earthwork revetments of the permanent HAA site built for urban defence. However, the vast majority of Suffolk's coastal HAA sites post-date the summer of 1944 and are of less substantial construction. This increase in construction rate and decrease in permanence reflects changing defensive strategies arising as a consequence of the invasion of Europe and Germany's introduction of the V1 flying bomb.

The Allied advance into France in 1944 denied the use of many airfields and V1 launch sites to the German forces, forcing them to launch from Holland and cross the British coastline over East Anglia. This caused the increasing number of somewhat makeshift HAA sites to be rapidly constructed in Suffolk. From the evidence visible on aerial photographs taken just after the war in 1945, it is apparent that these sites were of less durable construction than the example at Lowestoft, the gun emplacements very often composed simply of areas of hard-standing, possibly surrounded by sandbags or earthwork revetments. From July 1944, HAA on England's south coast was reorganised almost overnight to form what was known as the 'DIVER Belt', a gun zone established to combat the V1 threat. It is possible that not all of these sites even received guns before the next major strategic shift which affected Suffolk's artillery from September 1944.

From September 1944 the V1 launches shifted further to the north, resulting in a reorganisation of guns into a line from Clacton in Essex to Yarmouth in Norfolk; this was the DIVER strip and many of these DIVER sites have been recorded on the Suffolk coast. DIVER batteries can generally be distinguished from other HAA sites by the arrangement of gun emplacements into a straight line or flattened 'v' rather than an arc, the guns being laid out in this way to cross the flight path of the V1s and to allow the flanking guns to safely engage lower flying targets (see Figure 6b).

Some parts of the Suffolk coast, such as the area around Orford, have shown particularly dense concentrations of HAA and DIVER sites. In this area the date of the aerial photographs examined has shown that three batteries were constructed post 1943 and seven post May 1944, demonstrating that the majority were probably related to the institution of the DIVER strip.

The recording of these sites also illustrates the valuable role of aerial survey in complementing other survey methods. Comparison of the NMP plots and the site grid references recorded in the gazetteers of the HAA and DIVER volumes of the 20th Century Fortifications in England surveys by Dobinson (1996a, 1996c) shows some interesting patterns. The NMP survey has recorded three batteries not identified (Dobinson's comprehensive documentary survey and the aerial photographic evidence has improved the location of the sites by up to 200m in some cases. There are a number of possible reasons for this; it is possible that the DIVER sites on the research base at Orfordness remained unrecorded due to the secret nature of the work carried out there and the location of other sites may simply have been imprecisely recorded. Alternatively, local commanders may have adapted the original plans and ordered the construction

of sites in slightly more favourable locations. In addition, any inaccuracy in the original co-ordinates would have been compounded by conversion from the military Cassini Grid into National Grid co-ordinates. Such discrepancies once more highlight the value of the photographic resource in complementing the documentary evidence.

POTENTIAL BATTLEFIELD

Whilst researching this paper, a certain level of confusion in defining what constitutes a 'battlefield' became apparent. The significance of battlefields to British history is not in doubt and has been acknowledged by the creation of the Battlefields Register by English Heritage. However, all other factors that can be seen to define a battlefield, from its physical extent to its date are open to debate and are not necessarily applicable to the World War II defences of the Suffolk coast. For example, most authorities agree that battles are rarely stationary and range over the landscape (Newman 2003; Pollard and Oliver, 2002) but some permanent World War II anti-invasion defences on the Firth of Forth were included in a recent popular publication and television series on battlefield archaeology (Pollard and Oliver, 2002).

In his discussion of the nature of battlefields, Newman (2003) states that even apparently simple factors, such as the number of combatants and their military status, do not necessarily correlate with the social or political significance of a conflict's outcome. This is certainly the case for Suffolk's World War II coastal defences. For these reasons he suggests that the term 'place of conflict' may be preferable to 'battlefield'. In doing so, however, he argues that the physical act of combat, and the landscape which constrained or modelled it, gives rise to sets of 'values and significances' that are relevant to 'places of conflict' but not to 'facilities built to defend against attack, but which never saw combat' (Newman 2003, 38).

It would be illogical to suggest that a site which never saw conflict was a battlefield, but it also seems illogical to suggest that an entire landscape which was defended against ground, air and seaborne attack, a landscape armed to actively engage and destroy enemy forces, should be considered to have 'values and significances' of a lesser order than other places of conflict simply because it is of recent date and because particular elements have survived.

An important achievement of the Suffolk Coastal NMP project, in respect of the twentieth century defences, is therefore its success in placing the, often isolated, surviving remains into their wider wartime perspective, highlighting that importance does not directly correlate with permanence. The Suffolk coastal NMP project demonstrates that the isolated, surviving sites, the pillboxes and crumbling concrete coastal batteries, despite not seeing combat on the ground, represent the more ephemeral integrated defences' highest level of involvement in the conflict. For example, the project has re-established the connection between the surviving concrete anti-aircraft cubes, scattered across Orfordness, and the long since removed DIVER sites which shot down the last V1 of World War II.

In summarising the evidence from the Suffolk Coastal NMP project it is clear that although the Suffolk coast was not a battlefield in the traditional sense, it was undoubtedly directly involved in the conflict of World War II and was an important part of Britain's wider coastal anti-invasion landscape – what could be called a 'potential battlefield'. The NMP project has illustrated the integrated and interrelated nature of the home front defences on the Suffolk coast. Each site or structure may of itself not constitute a 'place of conflict', but viewed as a whole, the Suffolk coast during World War II was as much a 'landscape of conflict' as a landscape of defence, the surviving features the remains of possibly the greatest battlefield that never was.

FURTHER READING

M. Barber (forthcoming) Stonehenge from the air in 1900, The ballooning adventures of the Reverend John Mackenzie Bacon. *AARGNews* March 2005.

M. Barber, D. Grady, H Winton (2003) 'From pit circles to propellers: Recent results from Aerial Survey in Wiltshire' *Wiltshire Archaeological and Natural History Magazine* vol 96.

Crutchley S (2000) Salisbury Plain Training Area: A Report for the National Mapping Programme. *English Heritage internal report.*

Bewley, B. (2001) Understanding England's historic landscapes: an aerial perspective Landscapes 2:1, 74-84.

Defence of Britain (2002) A Review of the Defence of Britain project, *Council for British Archaeology,* **http://www.britarch.ac.uk/projects/dob/review/index.html**

Dobinson, C. (2001) *AA Command; Britain's Anti-Aircraft Defences of the Second World War.* Methuen, London.

Dobinson, C.S. (1998) *Twentieth-century fortifications in England: the MPP approach, in Monuments of War – the Evaluation, Recording and Management of Twentieth-century Military Sites,* ed. J. Schofield, English Heritage, London, 2-6.

Dobinson, C. (1996a) Operation DIVER – England's defence against the flying-bomb June 1944 – March 1945. Twentieth Century Fortifications in England IV York: *Council for British Archaeology.*

Dobinson, C. (1996b) Anti-invasion defences of WWII. Twentieth Century Fortifications in England II. York: *Council for British Archaeology.*

Dobinson, C. (1996c) Anti-aircraft artillery. Site Gazetteer, WWII HAA & ZAA. Twentieth Century Fortifications in England I.III York: *Council for British Archaeology.*

Fulford, M., Champion, T., & Long, A. (1997) *England's coastal heritage: a survey for English Heritage and the RCHME.* London: English Heritage.

Horne and Kershaw Forthcoming *'A Bold Flat...' Vale Of York NMP.* London: English Heritage.

Lowry, B. (1996) 20th Century defences in Britain: An introductory guide. York: *Council for British Archaeology.*

McOmish, Field and Brown (2002) The Field Archaeology of the Salisbury Plain Training Area

Newman, M. (2003) Why Fight for Battlefields? *Landscapes* 4:2, 34-41.

Newsome, S. (2003) The Coastal Landscape of Suffolk during the Second World War, *Landscapes* 4:2, 42-58

Wilson D (1982) *Air photo interpretation for archaeologists* London: Batsford (New edition 2000 Stroud: Tempus).

www.english-heritage.org.uk

THE AUTHORS

Cain Hegarty is a Survey Officer who, since 2001, has been working for Suffolk County Council on the Suffolk Coastal National Mapping Programme Project for English Heritage. With Sarah Newsome he has jointly authored articles and a report on various aspects of the Suffolk Coastal NMP project and is currently writing a book, with Sarah Newsome, on the military defences of the Suffolk coast from the air, due for publication late 2005/early 2006.

Sarah Newsome is an Investigator in the English Heritage Aerial Survey team in Swindon and has been working on the Suffolk Coastal National Mapping Programme Project for English Heritage since 2000.

Helen Winton has worked for Aerial Survey at English Heritage (formerly RCHME) for over ten years. This has involved projects throughout England, in particular in Lincolnshire, Wiltshire, the Lambourn Downs in Oxfordshire and Berkshire, and latterly the Areas of Natural Beauty in the Malvern and Quantock Hills. She currently manages the NMP projects for the south of England.

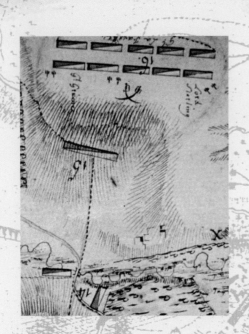

'If that park was where the 1778 battle took place, then why were Mike and I finding so much ordnance on the other side of the road?'

EVOLUTION OF MACRO-ARCHAEOLOGY OF THE BATTLE OF MONMOUTH - 1778 AMERICAN REVOLUTIONARY WAR

The Battle of Monmouth began when the Continental Army under George Washington took a cautious swipe at the rear of a British army marching from Philadelphia to New York. The British parried and thrust back. Washington took refuge on a hill behind an artillery line, beat back British attacks and won one of the largest battles of the American Revolution. Monmouth Battlefield is the first Revolutionary War battlefield ever to be fully excavated. For a dozen years, archaeologists and historians, most of them volunteers, have studied the archaeology, history, and mythology of the battle. Dan Sivilich was one of those who pioneered many of the procedures currently being used in battlefield archaeology today and below he reveals how evolving archaeological methods gave rise to new interpretations.

by Daniel M. Sivilich

BATTLEFIELDS POSE SIGNIFICANT LOGISTICS problems for archaeologists simply because most of them cover vast tracts of land due to the fluid movements of the opposing forces either attacking and/or retreating. Prior to the 20th century, many battles were fought by two armies forming straight battle lines and attacking one or another. This type of linear warfare required an open terrain typically unobstructed. A common source of land meeting these criteria was that found on farms. However, this further complicates issues for archaeologists. After the battles were over, the farmers continued with their livelihood and ploughed each site, disturbing the original artefact context, year after year, century after century. Ploughing also fosters another problem: relic hunting, both intentional and unintentional. The process of tilling the soil brings artefacts to the surface every season

'The lure of finding battlefield relics, whilst at the same time being encouraged to buy fresh farm produce, was a blatant marketing ploy.'

and exposes them to the elements. Rain washes the soil off and the artefacts then become visible.

Intentional relic hunters have been picking over battlefield sites from the day immediately following the battle to present times. This is done as a hobby as well as a business. At Monmouth Battlefield State Park in Freehold/Manalapan, New Jersey, site of a 1778 Revolutionary War battle, the local farmers advertised relic hunting on their farms as an added attraction for city people travelling to the area by train. The lure of finding battlefield relics, whilst at the same time being encouraged to buy fresh farm produce, was a blatant marketing ploy. With the current explosion of Internet sales, prices of military memorabilia have reached new heights. Coupled with the invention of and significant refinements in metal detectors, more and more sites are being destroyed in the hunt for valuable trophies. This has become a major problem even on 'protected' sites. Relic hunters - also called 'pot-hunters' - are willing to risk fines and arrest for the possibility of making a big score. However, there is also the unintentional relic hunter, or more accurately 'relic remover' and that is often the farmer. Larger ordnance such as cannon balls are sometimes picked up when observed and simply collected or discarded so that plough blades are not damaged if struck by the artefacts. In certain areas ordnance can be picked up by agricultural processing equipment such as potato picking machines. Whether intentional or not, the removal of artefacts obviously makes the archaeologist's job of locating a conflict site more difficult.

ARCHAEOLOGICAL NIGHTMARE

Many battles were fought using strategy rather than just brute force. This meant that when a dominant force began to gain ground, the opposing force would manoeuvre to try to gain a tactical advantage or would simply withdraw from the conflict. This often led to running battles or skirmishes creating a very large area of artefact distribution. These factors combined lead to an archaeological nightmare: the sites tend to be disturbed, very large and relic hunted.

Classical archaeological approaches dictate implementing a Cartesian coordinate system grid for a site and they employ a variety of techniques to evaluate the cultural resources. The 'quick and dirty' method is to sample the site with shovel tests. This is simply digging one-foot diameter holes at specific grid intersections and sifting the dirt through screens. The soil is typically removed in arbitrary levels of 3" - 6". Artefact distributions are then plotted, looking for specific loci of activity. Work done by Dr. Stephen Potter at Antietam revealed that the results of shovel tests at military conflict sites would be questionable even if large numbers of samplings were done (Potter, 1998). A more precise method of evaluating a site is by carefully excavating squares, typically 5' x 5' or 1m x 1m. The soils are carefully removed with trowels or flat shovels and the locations of artefacts are precisely recorded. This method is not practical due to the large areas covered by battles. A typical battlefield would require excavating thousands of squares. However, this technique is very useful in evaluating siege warfare sites in which the battle takes place in a fixed location such as in a fort, trenches or

'Whether intentional or not, the removal of artefacts obviously makes the archaeologist's job of locating a conflict site more difficult.'

specific buildings.

Finally, some battlefields become built over or significantly disturbed during phases of urbanization. A good example of this is the Battle of Princeton (3rd January 1777) in New Jersey. The actual preserved area is a few saved acres whereas the majority of the battlefield has been lost due to local housing, the growth of Princeton University and the Institute for Advanced Studies (working place of Albert Einstein). Only small segments of this significant event can, therefore be excavated and interpreted. The few areas that are left as open tracts of land are under threat of further building making any archaeological projects rushed; any salvage projects are thus only one step ahead of the bulldozers.

TROPHIES

Because of these problems, professional archaeologists had not attempted to excavate open terrain battlefields. As a result, no major battlefields were properly excavated prior to the 1980s. Yet many sites have been 'looted' since the 1960s by relic hunters brandishing metal detectors. This was especially true at American Civil War sites. A veritable cottage industry sprang up around this 'hobby' with magazines, relic hunting clubs, specialist digging tools and 'how-to' books. Rare military memorabilia were being sold, traded and proudly displayed as trophies rather than being treated as historical artefacts. Archaeological sites were being pilfered before they could be excavated. The situation almost reached a point where professional archaeologists began to regard anyone owning a metal detector as a looter and thief. Dr. David Starbuck was working on Rogers Island in the town of Fort Edward, New York. This was a significant American Revolutionary War camp and hospital site. Working with students and volunteers, Dr. Starbuck had cleared the topsoil from the site and left it for the following week to begin excavation of the exposed features. When he and the students returned the site resembled a lunar landscape with craters everywhere. Looters with metal detectors had hit the site heavily. Months of preparation and research were destroyed. What archaeological 'gems' were found and removed that week will never be known or recorded.

QUEST

In 1972 I bought my first metal detector. My objective was to find treasure, become rich and retire from my profession of Chemical Engineering. I had read about relic hunting, but frankly I did not have a significant interest in history. I took my detector to the New Jersey shore and found pocket change and an occasional piece of modern jewelry. I found enough to pay for upgrades to the next level of detector. After years of digging salt-corroded coins from the beaches, I found that hard ground sites such as older school playgrounds and parks produced older and higher quality coins. This was especially true for silver coins that did not oxidize or pit like copper coins. At last I was finding treasure. Now the quest became one of finding older coins. School playgrounds and parks generally yielded mid 19th century to 20th century coins. I joined a club and learned better techniques and also better locations to find older coins. Several years rolled by and I moved to Freehold, New Jersey and joined another club known as the Deep Search Metal Detecting Club. I learned that ploughed farm fields occasionally yielded 18th-century coins. They were not typically found in great numbers, but once in a great while a rarity would be found. Now my new quest began.

One day in 1987, I was driving by a farm field near my house and noticed the farmhouse was gone. I saw a person metal detecting the field so I stopped to enquire about the site. The man was Mike Kotza and he began to show me some lead musket balls he had found. I thought this could be a good site for coins. He indicated that the farm had been sold to a large corporation which was planning to put a research building on it. Until actual construction began, the property was leased to a local farmer, Charlie Wikoff. Mr. Wikoff had given Mike permission to metal detect on the land. I told him that I too was interested in the site and he simply told me that it was big enough for both of us. I took my metal detector from the car and began searching near Mike. Within a short time I had found nineteen musket balls but no coins. I was puzzled; across the street was Monmouth Battlefield State Park. If that park was where the 1778 battle took place, then why were Mike and I finding so much ordnance on the other side of the road? The engineer in me saw a problem that required a solution. First I realized that I would need my own permission to search the site. I contacted the company that owned the property and after numerous calls to different offices, found an official who said it was fine if I got permission from the farmer. After all, the site was ultimately designated for destruction by construction work. I contacted Charlie Wikoff, told him my

'I saw a person metal detecting the field so I stopped to enquire about the site. The man was Mike Kotza and he began to show me some lead musket balls he had found.'

intentions and asked his permission. He was quick to oblige since his wife Lydia was an enthusiastic local historian.

BAG, FLAG AND TAG

My engineering instincts and training immediately indicated that I should map what I found and look for patterns. I hand-sketched the site and began to plot artefact locations based on crude line-of-site positioning with structures, telephone poles and other features in the surrounding area. I noticed that the musket balls were either round or flattened from impact and seemed to come in different sizes. The diameters of the round balls could be measured easily, but the flattened ones posed a problem. Therefore, I decided to measure the gram weight of every artefact found. I observed that the musket balls seemed to cluster in three sizes if round or three weight categories if flattened. As I marked them on my crude map, patterns began to emerge of areas of specific concentrations. I had not found any 18th-century coins, but I was having fun playing detective in this 200 plus year old mystery. I invited a friend, Bernie Sorkin, to help me with metal detecting the site. After all, it was over 300 acres. Over time two Rangers, Nancy MacNeill and Bill Rainaud, working in the State Park would stop by out of curiosity and see what we were finding. We would show them our map and artefacts and discuss why so many artefacts were being found outside the State Park.

The site was very open and visible from a major highway and in a short period of time, other metal detectorists began to start digging at the site without permission. This became frustrating because we were losing data. I made the decision to ask for help from my friends at the Deep Search Metal Detecting Club. However, as I had come to view this as 'my site' I set down some ground rules. No one was allowed on the site unless I was present. All artefacts found were put into plastic bags with the date and name of the finder marked on each bag. They were to be left where they were found and the holes marked with plastic flags. Each artefact was then assigned a field identification number so that we could permanently associate it with its location. This system became known as "BAG, FLAG and TAG". At the end of every dig, I would map the artefact locations and collect the artefacts for measurement and recording. Since this was private property, legally we could keep the artefacts, but for some reason that just did not seem right to me. I told everyone that they could keep what they found, but it would be greatly appreciated if they would join me in donating them to an appropriate location. A significant number of artefacts were turned in for donation and we gave them to both Freehold Township and the Monmouth County Historical Association. Freehold Township in turn gave us an excellent topographical drawing of the site. This helped us refine our mapping techniques. In 1988 I met Ralph Phillips, a local avocational archaeologist who had extensive prehistoric knowledge. I taught him metal detecting and he taught me proper archaeological techniques.

I began mapping artefacts by classes. Each artefact class was assigned a distinct icon. Musket balls were sorted into nine classes. There were three size/weight categories and each of these were further broken down into three subclasses of round (probably never fired), deformed from impact after being fired, and chewed. We had found a few with teeth indentations in the lead. Our map began to show significant numbers of impacted musket balls indicating this was an area of intense conflict. However, if this was true, why was it not part of the State Park and being protected from destruction?

SYSTEMATIC SEARCH

In April of 1990, I was discussing this with Ranger Nancy MacNeill and she indicated that she wanted to introduce me to the new regional archaeologist, Garry Wheeler Stone. Garry was, at first, a little apprehensive at meeting with metal detectorists, but he was curious about our finds. When he saw our map and that each artefact was numbered and identified he was impressed. With assistance from people interested in other aspects of Monmouth Battlefield State Park, we formed a volunteer group. The Park encompassed nearly three square miles of property. Some of the land was leased to local farmers. This had a number of benefits. It provided the State with a small amount of revenue and preserved the battlefield's agricultural landscape. During 1990, an agricultural drain line ruptured during a torrential thunderstorm and eroded a five-foot deep gully. Filling the gully required the use of earth moving equipment that might displace or damage artefacts. Therefore, Garry requested that we conduct a controlled metal detecting survey of the field before the site was further disturbed. The field was small and did not take much time to sample. No military artefacts were found.

> I began mapping artefacts by classes. Each artefact class was assigned a distinct icon. Musket balls were sorted into nine classes.

Slightly northwest of the field was the Derrick Sutfin house. A section of this structure was built in approximately 1730 and was standing at the time of the 1778 battle. Bored with not finding anything, Ralph Phillips wandered out of the designated area into the farm field behind the house. Before we noticed he was gone, he found a musket ball. I did not know whether I should be angry or happy since I did not know what Garry Stone's reaction would be. Fortunately for battlefield archaeology, Garry was elated.

He devised a plan for the systematic metal detecting and excavation of the Sutfin site based on a Cartesian coordinate grid system. The entire field was laid out in 100' x 100' squares with re-bar posts at each grid corner. The grids would be systematically metal detected. When an artefact was found, its location was measured within the grid using X and Y coordinates. This data could then be mapped accurately on a base topographical map. At the time, we did not know that this technique had already been applied by Douglas D. Scott and Richard A. Fox, Jr. at the Little Bighorn National Park in 1984. Having a significant background in computer science, I wrote database software to manage the data but was also capable of sorting the information by many different variables for analysis. We also devised a plan to map the data on a computer. Evolution Computing in Tempe, Arizona was interested in our work and kindly donated FastCAD computer aided design software to the project. We had a topographical map of the park professionally scanned in a CAD format. I georeferenced the map and we were ready to begin plotting data, but I needed a better way to classify musket balls. The volume of a sphere is a function of its diameter, and the weight of a sphere is a function of its volume and its density. If I knew the density of the lead used in the musket balls, I could create a simple formula to calculate the original diameter of a deformed musket ball. However, I could not assume the density of pure elemental lead. I did not know the effects of impurities, trapped air and the surface patina. Therefore, I needed to reverse engineer the density of 18th century musket ball lead. The best way to do this was to measure the diameters and weights of spherical musket balls that had been excavated and calculate the density. Once I had done that, it was easy to devise a formula to calculate musket ball diameters:

Diameter of lead sphere in inches = 0.223204 x (Weight in grams)$^{1/3}$.

Now we had the ability to classify musket balls on our map by diameter rather than weight. Obviously the diameter of a musket ball is proportional to the bore of the gun. It now became possible to identify troop locations by the ordnance being used by them and being dropped or fired at them by the opposing force. Musket balls were now grouped by diameter as follows:

Less than 0.60" diameter - typical for 18th century rifles. 0.60" - 0.66" diameter - mid-range smooth bore musket such as the French Charleville and the British fusil. Greater than 0.66" diameter - large smooth bore muskets, typically associated with British Brown Bess muskets.

Specific CAD layers were designated for each of the artefact classifications. These layers could be viewed individually or in groups as will be shown later in this paper. We now had a viable system for evaluating a large battlefield which we call macro-archaeology. By looking at large areas such as 40 - 50 acre segments, agriculturally disturbed sites become interpretable. Artefact movement of several feet caused by ploughing, animal burrow and soil erosion for example, may be significant when looking at a 5' x 5' square, but when viewing 40 acres on a computer screen, this can represent a single pixel or less. The size of the area also nullifies measuring errors described in the next section. However, there were still some shortcomings that needed refinement.

The 100' x 100' grid system was a logistical problem. The re-bar corner markers had to be removed every spring before the farmer could plow. If left in the field, they can puncture very expensive tractor tires. The grid would then have to be re-established every fall after the crops were harvested. Again being an engineer, I knew there was more than one way to locate a point on a plane. The other method is known as the Polar coordinate system. Instead of X (horizontal measurement) and Y (vertical measurement), it used X (distance measurement) and an angle from a known reference line. In our case, the reference line chosen was magnetic north. So by having a known point or benchmark with X, Y coordinates, the location of another point could be established by measuring the distance and compass bearing from the benchmark. CAD systems can plot points in either type of coordinate system. We surveyed points around the perimeters of the fields in unploughed areas and established a permanent benchmark system. At the end of the day it was significantly faster to measure in artefact locations from these perimeter points. However, if artefacts were found beyond the length of our tape measure (300') then the

measurement would have to be taken in two steps. This could introduce a small amount of error. Although this system works reasonably well for disturbed sites, compass measurements can have small errors due to local magnetic variations throughout a field. Another small error is introduced since the tape measure is run parallel to the ground which does not yield the true horizontal distance that would be plotted on a two dimensional topographic map. Again in a disturbed site, this error is not significant. However, through grants and donations, we were able to secure a Trimble total station laser transit. Now true survey measurements can be taken over great distances to yield the actual coordinates, horizontal distances and elevation of an artefact location with sub-centimeter accuracy.

DATA MAPPING

Newer software has become available and is referred to as Geographic Information Systems (GIS) that is designed specifically for mapping data. ESRI Inc., kindly donated ArcView to our organization and the Monmouth County GIS Office donated the aerial photographs and associated topographic data for the battlefield. Now the artefacts are excavated, the data measured and collected with the total station, the data is downloaded into our field laptop computer and ArcView imports the data onto a georeferenced aerial photograph of the site before we leave the field. All of this evolved from a hand-sketch map on which artefacts were located by their rough proximity to a nearby telephone pole, hilltop or tree.

The results of our surveys in the Park have led to a complete reanalysis of the Battle of Monmouth and a new and accurate interpretation has emerged.

Our group has evolved as well. We are now known as the Battlefield Restoration and Archaeological Volunteer Organization, BRAVO for short. And what happened to the original farm that we discovered was the site of a major conflict? It was rescued from destruction based on our data, acquired by the State and incorporated into the Monmouth Battlefield State Park. The results of our surveys in the Park have led to a complete reanalysis of the Battle of Monmouth and a new and accurate interpretation has emerged. We have learned that the battle was very fluid and complex. The remainder of this article will demonstrate how the archaeological data was used to reconstruct one segment of the battle.

THE BATTLE OF MONMOUTH

The winter of 1777 - 1778 was particularly harsh for the American army camped at Valley Forge whilst the

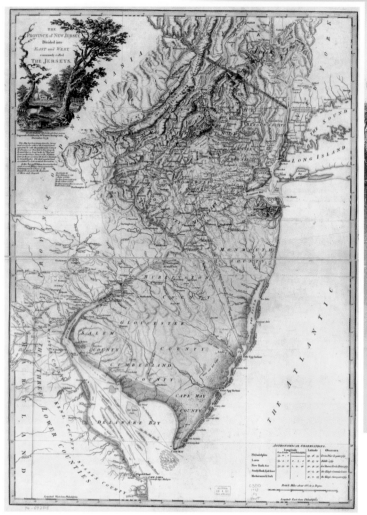

Figure 1 - Map of 'The Province of New Jersey, Divided Into East and West Commonly Called the Jerseys', December 1778

Figure 2 - Anonymous Molly.

British spent the winter in the warmth and hospitality of the city of Philadelphia. However, the French entered the war on the American side and in the spring of 1778 General Sir Henry Clinton, Commander of the Crown Forces, feared that the French Navy might blockade the harbour. As a safeguard, he decided to move his army to New York. Equipment and supplies were loaded on board British Navy ships and sent to New York. The army of some 21,000 troops, civilian workers, loyalist units and camp followers were marched across the 'Jerseys' towards New York (Figure 1).

General George Washington, Commander of the American forces, led a Continental Army of about 13,000 men across New Jersey to intercept the British. Wanting to avoid a major battle with the larger British army, Washington sent an advance force to stage a demonstration against the British line of march. On

26th June the British reached the town of Monmouth Courthouse (today known as Freehold). There they rested. Washington and most of the American army were in Cranbury, New Jersey and posed no threat. As the Crown Forces rested, however, the American advance guard arrived at Englishtown on 27th June. Now the armies were only a few miles apart. On the morning of 28th June, Washington ordered an attack on the British rear and the Battle of Monmouth began.

From folk memories of the battle grew two myths: one of patriotism and courage triumphing over cowardice and treachery. The other of the courage of the American woman as represented by Molly Pitcher, the 'woman at the gun' (Figure 2). Since the Centennial, Molly has been one of the all-American icons that have kept food on the tables of a multitude of artists and publishers. These images are mere symbols (Figure 3), sometimes ridiculous (Figure 4). Note how this particular Molly is about to be run-down as the gun she is firing recoils.

In his memoir, Joseph Plumb Martin, a Connecticut private, writes of watching a woman run cartridges to a loader, 'attending the piece the whole time':

'We had a four-pounder on the left of our pieces which kept a constant fire on the enemy . ... A woman . . . attended with her husband at the piece the whole time. While in the act of

Figure 3 - Humorous Molly.   *Figure 4 - Ridiculous Molly.*

reaching a cartridge and having one of her feet as far before the other as she could step, a cannon shot from the enemy passed directly between her legs without doing any other damage than carrying away the lower part of her petticoat.'

JOSEPH PLUMB MARTIN, 8TH CONNECTICUT

Martin implies that this was a light field piece, one that fired a four-pound projectile, a piece at the left end of the Continental gun line. Through battlefield archaeology, we appear to have located this gun position.

THE SUTFIN FARM

The Battle of Monmouth was one of the largest and longest land battles of the War for American Independence. It was a fluid battle, traversing almost 20 miles. So where does one begin to find the Battle of Monmouth? Figure 5 shows the 1778 Simcoe map of the battle. This was a British map and since the British left the field of battle, the map must have been drawn from memory since the topography and land features are not accurate.

Figure 6 shows a section of the 1778 map by Michel Capitaine du Chesnoy, cartographer for the Marquis de Lafayette. Since the Americans took the field, this map was probably drawn by eye and is a good representation of the terrain. Questions remain, however, regarding the accuracy of troop dispositions and movements.

Figure 5: Lieutenant Colonel John Simcoe's watercolour of the Battle of Monmouth.

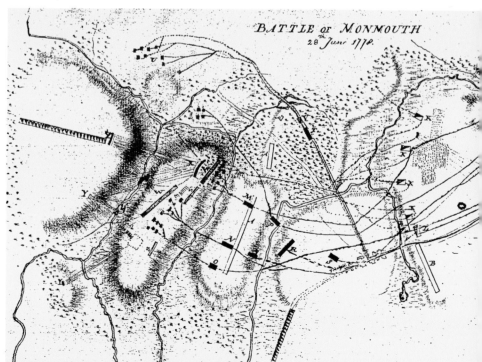

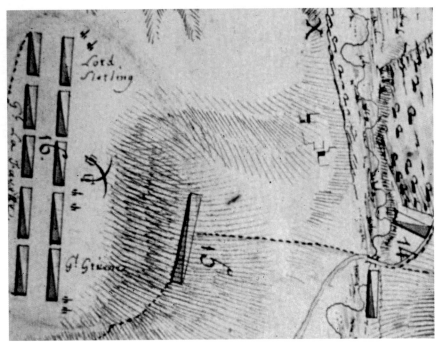

Figure 6 - Section of the Capitaine Map.

One segment of the Battle of Monmouth that took place on the Derick Sutfin farm between the 42nd Regiment of Foot and a group of Continental soldiers from New England is examined below to demonstrate how the archaeological results were analyzed and interpreted. The large 'X' to the top right in Figure 6 represents the location of the 42nd. The Sutfin house, barn and outbuildings are the small rectangles below the 'X'.

Figure 7 is a contemporary aerial view of the same area of the Capitaine map. Although the road has been straightened, much of the terrain and view shed is the same as it was in 1778.

Figure 8 is a current topographical map of the site. By plotting all military artefacts, it becomes readily apparent that this is where the New Englanders clashed with the Royal Highlanders, but this data is difficult to interpret and does not distinguish any specific details about the battle.

Figure 7 - Current aerial view of site.

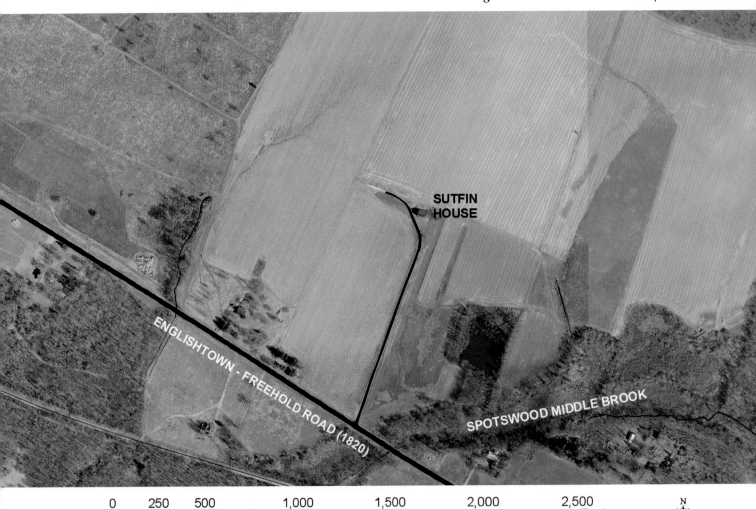

SUTFIN HOUSE

ENGLISHTOWN - FREEHOLD ROAD (1820)

SPOTSWOOD MIDDLE BROOK

0   250   500   1,000   1,500   2,000   2,500
Feet

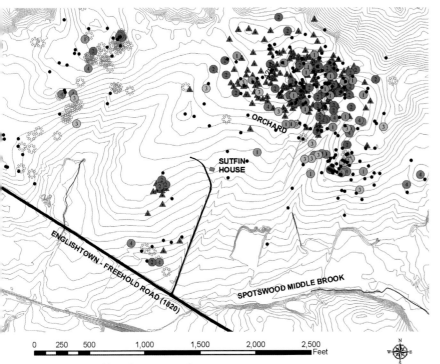

Figure 8 – All military artefacts.

By organizing artefact classes into GIS layers and viewing these layers individually specific events, and sometimes features, can be isolated. Using a combination of historical text and this archaeological data, the battle between the American New England troops and the 42nd Regiment of Foot began to unfold.

GRAPESHOT AND CANISTER - LOCATING THE APPLE ORCHARD

The British 3rd Brigade divested themselves of their packs and crossed Spotswood Middle Brook in an attempt to flank the American line. They moved west until they were spotted by the American artillery and a barrage of canister and grapeshot stopped their advance. The 1st Battalion of the Royal Highlanders and another regiment (44th) swung north, while the 2nd Battalion of the Highlanders, the 42nd Regiment of Foot (decades later known as the Black Watch) hunkered down in an apple orchard. Figure 9 shows a potential location for the orchard, but is it correct? Can historical document research and archaeology locate the missing orchard?

When people think of cannons firing, they think of cannon balls flying through enemy lines. However, cannon balls were not very effective anti-personnel ordnance. Cannons could be used like giant shotguns using special scatter shot. The American artillery opened fire with 2-ounce grapeshot and lead canister shot. The Highlanders took cover in a swale in Derick Sutfin's cider orchard. The location of this orchard can be identified by the cluster of ordnance excavated as shown

in Figure 10. The data shows that the Americans' aim into the orchard was accurate.

Grapeshot is a cluster of iron balls in a linen sack. When fired from a cannon the bag burnt off and the balls scattered like the pellets from a giant shotgun. This was a very effective anti-personnel weapon. The data shows more than just the impact locations of the grapeshot. Figure 11 shows a cluster of grape excavated at the American artillery line. The American guns were out of range for British grapeshot. However, if the canvas sack ripped, the shot could spill out as we see with this cluster of 4 pieces. They are all 2-ounce balls probably from the same round. This gives us a very good indication of the actual location of the artillery piece. The historical text indicates this to be in the vicinity of Proctor's Artillery ... the gun attended to by Molly.

Fortunately, we have a Continental account that connects the 'woman who attended the piece' with a Continental artillery unit. A physician wrote of watching Washington admire 'the manner in which Proctor was handling' the enemy right. It is interesting to note that

Figure 9 - The 42nd Regiment of Foot in Orchard.

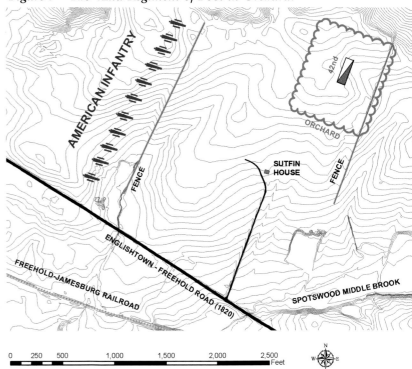

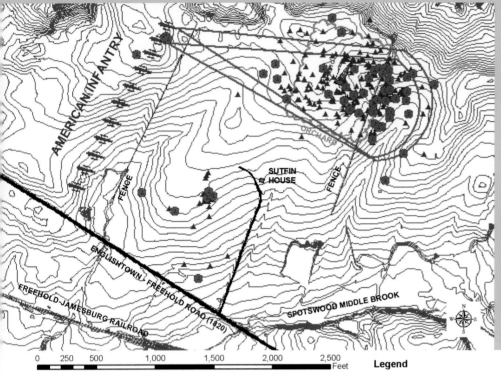

Figure 11- above: Cluster of dropped 2-ounce grapeshot.

Figure 10 - left: Locations of excavated 2-ounce grapeshot and lead canister shot.

Legend

● Grape 2 oz   ▲ Canister

Mary Hays, the woman most often connected with the Molly Pitcher myth, was the wife of a gunner in Captain Francis Proctor's artillery company.

> '*He saw Washington standing to the right of the line, . . . and saw a cannon ball strike a wet hole in the side of the hill, and the dirt fly on him. The General, coolly standing in his stirrups, was said to say to the officers who urged that that was no place for him, he being observed by the enemy, . . . "that he was admiring the manner in which Proctor was handling their right."'*

DR. WILLIAM READ

Figure 12 - Examples of canister shot fused from the force of impact. PHOTO BY MICHAEL F. SMITH

Canister shot is a tin can filled with lead musket balls. It does not necessarily rupture upon exiting the muzzle of a cannon. Therefore, it is fired at a low, flat angle to hit the ground approximately 75 yards in front of the enemy. The can ruptures as it glances off the ground and lead balls and earthen debris are thrown into the enemy ranks. The force of this impact is so great that it often fuses the shot together, as in Figure 12.

ARTILLERY DUEL

While the 42nd was in the orchard, the American and British artillery bombarded each other intensely for several hours. This was the longest and largest field artillery duel of the Revolutionary War. The British had two 5 1/2" howitzers that they fired accurately into the American artillery line. Shell fragments rained down on the American position, but the historical texts do not indicate any great level of casualties. However, the locations of these artefacts, when plotted onto the GIS maps, confirm the location of this artillery line as shown in Figure 13.

Howitzers were short-barreled artillery pieces that were capable of firing at higher elevations than standard cannons. They could lob a projectile over an enemy fortification. Howitzer shells were hollow cast iron balls filled with black powder and had a fuse timed to explode the shell inside the enemy position. The shell would fragment into a multitude of sharp cast iron projectiles that could inflict serious injury or damage.

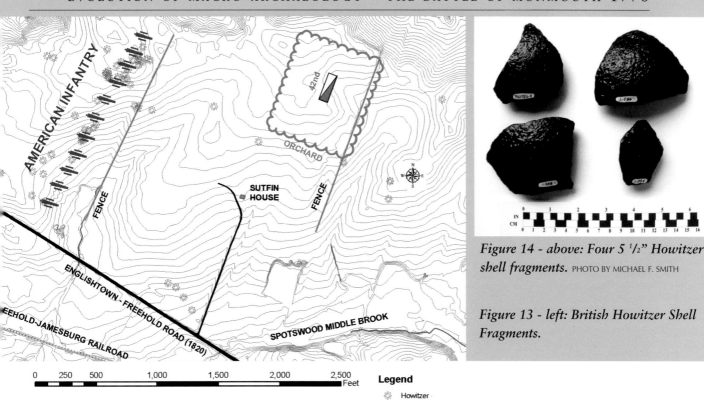

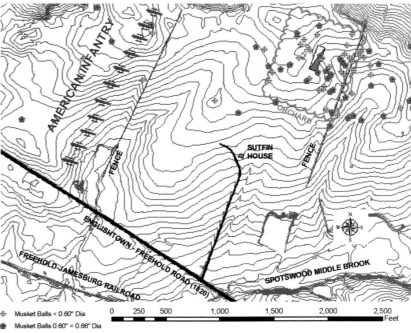

Legend

❀ Howitzer

Figure 14 - above: Four 5 ¹/₂" Howitzer shell fragments. PHOTO BY MICHAEL F. SMITH

Figure 13 - left: British Howitzer Shell Fragments.

Figure 14 shows several howitzer shell fragments excavated from the American artillery position. Note that their glossy appearance is due to the artefacts being conserved to prevent future rusting and deterioration.

SNIPER FIRE

The archaeological work shows that the men of the 42nd Regiment faced sniper fire from the north. Figure 15 shows the locations where impacted musket balls were excavated. Based on their locations (in the orchard area) and the two ranges of diameters, it can be concluded that these musket balls were fired by the Americans at the Highlanders. Based on the work done by BRAVO, musket balls are grouped into three basic diameter ranges. Less than 0.60" in diameter are typically used by rifles. 0.60" - 0.66" can encompass a variety of smooth bore muskets, but are most commonly associated with French Charleville muskets - supplied by France to America - and British fusils. Greater than 0.66" in diameter are usually associated with large fowling pieces and military issue British Brown Bess muskets. Based on the data, the British were not using rifles at Monmouth, but the majority of impacted musket balls in the orchard area were from rifles. Rifles took a greater amount of time to load than smooth bore muskets, and were therefore not preferred as combat weapons. However, they were significantly more accurate than muskets and were preferred by snipers.

SLUGGS

Cylindrical shot were also being fired at the Highlanders in the orchard. A Continental sniper altered round musket balls by hammering them into cylinders or 'Sluggs'. This is equivalent to modern, illegal 'dum-dum' bullets. This shot would tumble after firing and rip

Figure 15 - Impacted musket balls (less than 0.60˝ and 0.60˝ - 0.66˝ diameter).

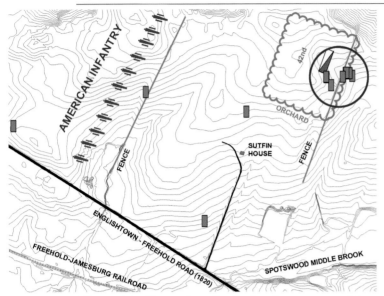

Figure 16 - Examples of cylinder shot excavated in the orchard site.

through human targets causing massive, irreparable injury.

The GIS data shows the accuracy at which these sluggs were being fired. With such tight patterns we might envision an intended target. Such determined fire might suggest a Highland officer was being sighted. The question was raised as to what type of weapon was being used to fire these sluggs.

They were all hammered down to a diameter of less than 0.60" in diameter suggesting that they may have been altered to fit a rifle. Could it simply be that a rifleman ran out of ammunition and took larger musket balls and made them fit his weapon? We thought we had something very unique. However, the use of cylindrical shot is not unique to Monmouth and appears to have a long history. Five specimens were excavated from the pirate ship Whydah which sank off Cape Cod in 1717.

Lieutenant Colonel Henry Dearborn, 3rd New Hampshire.

The shot were found in the same leather pouch with 23 round musket balls. An analysis of the calculated diameters of the cylindrical shot, using the above formula, shows they were all made from 0.63" diameter musket balls. This strongly suggests that they were for the same smooth bore musket as the round shot. Therefore, it is concluded that a Continental sniper was firing the sluggs from a musket at Monmouth.

CILLEY'S 'PICKED MEN'

Having failed to breach the Continental Army defences, the British Commander began to withdraw. Washington seized the opportunity to launch another limited attack, sending two battalions of light infantry to attack the Highlanders in the orchard. In front were 350 New Englanders under the command of Colonel Joseph Cilley.

"His excellency ordered me to take the battalion that I commanded, consisting of 350 rank and file, . . . to go and see what I could do with the enemy's right wing, which was formed in an orchard in our front."

COLONEL JOSEPH CILLEY, 1ST NEW HAMPSHIRE - 22ND JULY 1778

Threatened on two sides, the Highlanders quickly filed off. They withdrew south through the orchard and along the fence line. The Continentals pursued in formation. Colonel Cilley realized quickly that his battalion - formed in line and, hampered by trees and fences – could not overtake the Highlanders. So he dispatched men to run after the Highlanders in an attempt to slow their withdrawal.

'Colonel Cilley, finding that we were not likely to overtake the enemy . . . on account of fences and other obstructions, ordered three or four platoons from the right of our corps to pursue and attack them, and thus keep them in play till the rest of the detachment could come up. I was in this party; we pursued without order. As I passed through the orchard, I saw a number of the enemy lying under the trees, killed by our fieldpiece, mentioned before.'

JOSEPH PLUMB MARTIN, 8TH CONNECTICUT

The skirmishers caught up to the Highlanders as they formed on a hill to fire at their pursuers. No document records the skirmishers' fire, but the evidence, in the form of impacted musket balls, survived in the ground. By looking at the two layers of smaller diameter impacted musket balls in Figure 16, one can clearly see the location of the 42nd when it was fired on by the American skirmishers.

'The enemy, when we were taking down the last fence, gave us a very heavy fire which we did not return. We marched on with arms shouldered .... The enemy finding we were determined to close with them filed off from the left and run off upon our right into a swamp and formed in the edge of it. We wheeled to the right and advanced towards them. They began a heavy fire upon us.'

LIEUTENANT COLONEL HENRY DEARBORN, 3RD NEW HAMPSHIRE.

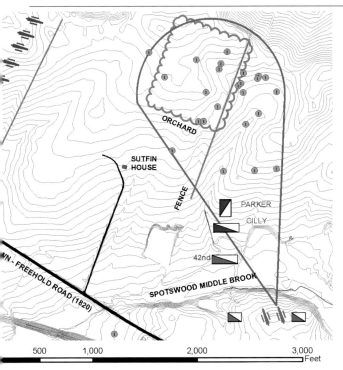

Figure 17 - The 42nd withraws, covered by supporting fire from two 'grasshoppers'.

BITING THE BULLET

After firing at the New Englanders, the Highlanders filed off again. The Continentals wheeled their line to follow. As they did so, the British opened fire with two 'grasshoppers' - lightweight 3-pounders - held back to cover the Highlanders' withdrawal. The first shot killed two men from Lexington, MA, and wounded a third. Archaeology revealed that the British were firing 1 or 1¼ ounce case shot as shown in Figure 17.

With shouldered muskets, the Continental light infantry marched steadily into heavy fire from the Highlanders. When at point-blank range, the Continentals began firing, advancing with levelled bayonets between volleys. Finding that the Continentals were determined to close, the Highlanders broke off, crossed the brook, and joined their main body.

'When our commander saw them retreating and nearly joined with their main body, he shouted, "Come, my boys, reload your pieces, and we will give them a set-off." We did so, . . . and the firing on both sides ceased. We then laid ourselves down under the fences and bushes to take breath, for we had need of it. I presume everyone has heard of the heat of that day, but none can realize it that did not feel it. Fighting is hot work in cool weather, how much more so in such weather as it was on the twenty-eighth of June, 1778.'

JOSEPH PLUMB MARTIN, 8TH CONNECTICUT

The fighting on the Continental left was over. No longer able to pursue, Cilley's light infantry rested. The more mercenary looted the dead Highlanders; the more compassionate tended to the wounded. Human chewed musket balls have been found on the battlefield to identify the location of the wounded. By this time the Battle of Monmouth was over and Washington and the American army claimed a much needed victory. Martin, however, describes the battlefield having a number of wounded soldiers scattered about. Martin helped one back to Tennent Meeting House which served as a hospital. Archaeology indicates that some may have been tended in the field. Anaesthetics were not yet invented. Officers may have been given some rum if it was available. Lowly privates were simply given a lead ball or a stick to bear down on while a limb was amputated in the field. This prevented them from biting their tongues or breaking their teeth. Thus the term 'Bite the Bullet' was born.

Our fieldwork at Monmouth is continuing. Field surveys continue and more artefacts are being collected for physical analysis. The data is added to the GIS maps and new discoveries are still being made. The interpretation of the Battle of Monmouth has changed significantly and important event locations are being marked with wayside exhibits for self-guided tours of the Park.

REFERENCES:

Potter, Stephen 1998 Towels and Technology: How to Survey a Battlefield. Paper Presented at the Fourth National Conference on Battlefield Preservation, sponsored by The American Battlefield Protection Program, Charleston, SC.

Scott, Douglas D. and Richard A. Fox Jr. 1989 *Archaeological Insights into the Custer Battle*. Fifth Edition. Reprint of 1987 edition. University of Oklahoma Press, Norman.

Scott, Douglas D., Richard A. Fox Jr., Melissa A. Connor and Dick Harmon.1989 *Archaeological Perspectives on the Battle of the Little Bighorn*. University of Oklahoma Press, Norman.

Sivilich, Daniel M. 1995 The Archaeology of the Battle of Monmouth: Chapter 2 - The Repulse of the British 3rd Brigade. Paper Presented at the Conference on Underwater and Historical Archaeology, Society for Historical Archaeology, Washington, DC.

Sivilich, Daniel M. 1996 Analyzing Musket Balls to Interpret a Revolutionary War Site. *Historical Archaeology* 30 (2), pp.101-109.

Sivilich, Daniel M., Garry Wheeler Stone 2003 'The Archaeology of Molly Hays and Joseph Plumb Martin,' *New Jersey Heritage Magazine*, Vol. 2, No. 2 (Spring 2003), pp.30-34.

Stone, Garry Wheeler, Daniel M. Sivilich and Mark Edward Lender. A Deadly Minuet: The Advance of the New England 'Picked Men' against the Royal Highlanders at The Battle of Monmouth. *The Brigade Dispatch*, Volume 26, No. 2, Brigade of the American Revolution, River Vale, NJ.

MUSEUM PIECE

CRYER FARM: EXCAVATION AND RESTORATION OF A WWI GERMAN DRESSING STATION ON THE YPRES-MENIN ROAD

By Franky Bostyn MA, Curator Memorial Museum Passchendaele 1917 and Chairman Association for Battlefield Archaeology in Flanders (ABAF)

SINCE 1999 THE ASSOCIATION for Battlefield Archaeology in Flanders has been working on a systematic inventory of all WWI bunkers on the former battlefields around Ypres. During a detailed survey of the village of Gheluvelt, now a part of Zonnebeke, we came across an underground German bunker that was completely overgrown and inaccessible. The landowners, the Bauden family, knew only that it had been partially cleaned out in May 1940 as a shelter for local inhabitants and that it was then used as a large cesspool for the adjoining farm until 1985. As the owners also wanted to know what they had actually got in their garden an archaeological excavation was undertaken in December 2001. The bunker proved to be so impressive and in such an excellent state that an agreement was made to restore it. In the meantime thorough historical research was undertaken to determine the origins of the underground complex. The site was officially opened to the public in November 2002 and since then has received several thousand visitors.

'The bunker proved to be so impressive and in such an excellent state that an agreement was made to restore it.'

A 1916 GERMAN DRESSING STATION

Cryer Farm is located 320 metres to the east of what was an important crossroads on the Ypres-Menin Road, known during WW1 as Clapham Junction. At 64 metres above sea level it was one of the highest points in the Ypres Salient - higher than Hill 62 and Hill 60. This site is approximately 1500 metres from the 1915-17 front line trenches at Hooge and 250 metres in front of the second German line or Albrecht-Stellung. It is also between the important communication trenches *Geyerweg* (Jargon Drive) and *Meissengasse* (Jap Avenue), to which it is connected. From the frontline at Hooge a light railway track ran in the direction of Nonnebossen, than crossed the Oude Kortrijkstraat (the old Ypres-Courtrai road) to end on the main Ypres-Menin Road where it connected with the pre-war tramway. The Decauville line was used to bring up men and material to the front and to evacuate the wounded.

It was for the latter purpose that in 1916 a first aid dressing station was built along the railway line. This was not a regimental aid post, casualty clearing station or field hospital, but simply a place where wounded were selected and made ready for further transport to the actual hospitals in Menin.

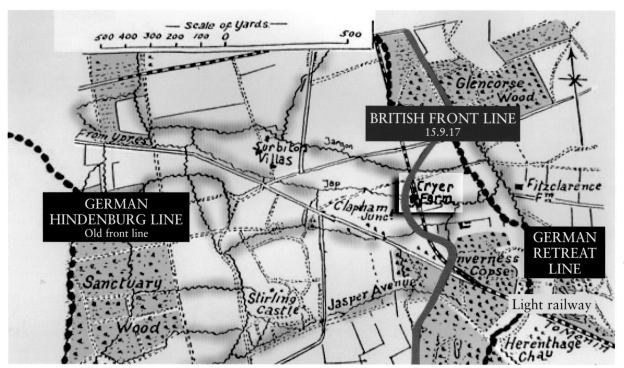

Cryer Farm, the Albrecht-Stellung, Clapham Junction and the Hooge-Menin Road light railway. MMP17

We have no exact references to the actual building of the dressing station but it certainly dates back to 1916, when most of these constructions were undertaken. We found references in two German regimental histories about dressing stations north of the Menin Road; Grenadier-Regiment 119 in the spring of 1916 and Reserve-Infantry-Regiment 209 in December 1916. The *grosser neuer Sanitätsunterstand am Geierweg vor der II, Stellung,* as described in the RIR 209 history, is probably the Cryer Farm bunker.

About 250 metres to the east of the bunker a German Cemetery was in existence with 412 burials. Ehrenfriedhof No. 47 (Hooge) was closed in 1955 and the remains moved to Langemarck and Menin.

SECOND LIEUTENANT BERNARD NOEL CRYER

Due to the British advances during the Third Battle of Ypres, the Germans transformed their dressing station into a heavily defended strongpoint. On the 15th September 1917, a raiding party of the 7th Battalion London Regiment (47th Division), a party which included Second Lieutenant

Cryer Farm as it is today. The pre-war farm buildings were in the meadow between the actual farm and the tree on the right. ABAF

Bernard Noel Cryer, was detailed to capture the bunker. In the official history of the 47th Division, Alan Maude detailed the following:

After carefully studying the ground for several nights before by means of patrols, the raiding party, under cover of a hurricane artillery barrage, rushed the post, killed ten of the enemy and captured thirty-six prisoners and a Machine Gun with comparatively light casualties. This operation earned the troops concerned the praise of the Army and Corps Commanders, who considered it a really first-class piece of work. An enemy counter-attack against this newly-established post, which had been consolidated, was driven off early in the morning of the 16th, with heavy losses to the enemy, but the gallant Cryer, to the regret of all, was killed. In his memory the captured post was named Cryer Farm.

Jan Vancoillie identified the German unit involved as the 4th Company of Bavarian Reserve-Infantry-Regiment No. 4.

In 2003 Andy Cryer, great-grandson of Second Lieutenant Noel Cryer, heard about the Cryer Farm bunker being opened to the public. He made contact with the museum and provided family information about Second Lieutenant Cryer. The body of Second Lieutenant Cryer was never recovered. He is commemorated on panels 52-54 of the Menin Gate Memorial to the Missing in Ypres.

Second Lieutenant Bernard Noel Cryer and a card printed by his family on his death. A CRYER

Copy of Telegram received from Buckingham Palace.

"The King and Queen deeply regret the loss you and the army have sustained by the death of your husband in the service of his country. Their Majesties truly sympathise with you in your sorrow."
Keeper of the Privy Purse.

"You have doubtless heard by this time of the sad news of the death of 2nd Lieut. B. N. Cryer. Please accept my very deep sympathy in the great loss you have sustained. He was killed on September 15th, 1917, during the capture of Cryer Farm (named after him as he was the only officer to reach the post). He was a capable and efficient officer, popular with all ranks, and will be greatly missed by his men."
Major-General,
Commanding 47th (London) Division.

"His death fills me with the greatest regret, both because I have lost a most capable and promising officer and also on personal grounds. He was loved by all his comrades, both officers and men, and was a credit to himself and to his regiment. He was specially selected to command a party of sixty men to raid and take a strong point which, while it remained in German hands, seriously impeded the attack which was to be made on September 20th. The operation was made at 4 p.m. on September 15th, and was brilliantly successful. Its success was largely due to his careful study of the preliminary arrangements and his skilful leading on the day. To the great regret of everyone he was killed instantaneously by a shell at the moment of victory. He was buried by his comrades on the ground which he had captured, and a cross erected over his grave. It may be some consolation to you to know that he captured has been his success the strong point which he captured has been officially called "Cryer's Farm." An instantaneous death could have been happier than his. An instantaneous death without any suffering in the moment of victory, when he knew victory had been obtained. You have every right to be proud of him. He was a thoroughly capable soldier, and had been marked out as one on whom reliance could be placed, and to whom higher responsibilities than those of Second Lieutenant could be entrusted. He would not have remained a Second Lieutenant much longer had fate been propitious. I feel his loss on personal grounds very much indeed. He was a charming boy, and if all subalterns were as keen, capable and pleasant as he was, a Commanding Officer's duties would be much less arduous."
Commanding Officer,
1/7th Batt. London Regt., France.

BERNARD NOEL CRYER

2nd Lieutenant 7th London Regiment.

BORN DECEMBER 25TH, 1892.

Enlisted in 7th London Regiment, September 4th, 1914.
Gazetted to the above Regiment, March 1st, 1917.

KILLED IN ACTION AT "CRYER'S FARM," YPRES,
SEPTEMBER 15TH, 1917.

"His heart to his home, his soul to his God,
his life for his country."

MRS. BERNARD CRYER, MR. and MRS. WALTER CRYER and MR. and MRS. C. E. EBBON wish to return thanks for the kind sympathy they have received in their great loss.

"Helvétia,"   117 Mount View Road,
Haringey Park,   Stroud Green,
Crouch End,   London, N.4.
London, N.8.

"Although he was only in my Company a short time he gained the love of all his brother officers, also all the men of his platoon. His death was instantaneous, and he carried out the task he was detailed to perform with the greatest of success, showing great skill and gallantry. I feel his loss very greatly, as he was a Sergeant in my Platoon in 1916, and also that I shall not be able to replace him."
Captain,
1/7th London Regiment, France.

"Everyone speaks extremely highly of the manner in which he carried the raid through. He did his job well, and his death was painless, and furthermore, he was properly buried. Believe me, I personally cannot say how I feel his death, having known him, and to have known him was to have admired him greatly."
A Brother Officer.

"From what I know of his character, and judging from numerous letters that I had from him since he came out here, I am sure that he was happy to be fighting at last. After so many months of training he seemed to be glad of the opportunity to put it all to the test, and to judge from his letters, it was a great and joyous realisation to him to discover how well and easily he was able to endure the dangers and shoulder the many responsibilities that came his way. The devotion of his men and the friendship of his fellow officers was, I know, another great source of happiness to him, and his charming personality always made him a general favourite. Always kind and considerate, and modest almost to a fault, it was only he himself who doubted his own abilities. I think that he was without doubt the favourite N.C.O. of his Company, and indeed he could do more with the men than most of the Sergeants."
His chum Officer, 8th Royal Scots, France.

AN EXCEPTIONAL BUNKER

The dimensions of the underground constructions are 16.8 x 7.1 metres, built in two blocks with a gallery between. The entrance blocks are concreted on temporary wooden frameworks, the latter on typical steel sheets, similar to the British elephant sheets. These are built opposite each other and give an internal width of 3 metres at ground level. The steel sheets are still

Plan of Cryer Farm. ABAF

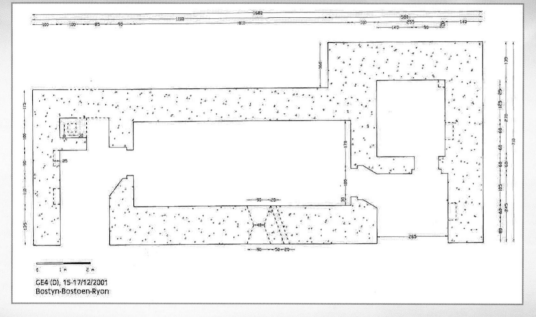

preserved, but heavily corroded due to its use as a cesspool. The thickness of the roof above the main entrance bunker is 1.3m in reinforced concrete, which is amongst the heaviest in the area.

The Cryer Farm bunker has a remarkable drainage system with two sumps, one in each of the entrance blocks. The southernmost sump is the major one as the main gallery has a slight slope down to it. There are many traces of the original tar roofing which sealed the roof to prevent leakage from the surface.

The east side of the gallery has a remarkable, double conical window-opening and a stove pipe. Both entrance-blocks have an air vent through the roof, of which the southernmost is in a special room of 1.00 x 0.70 metres, where the remains of a stove were found. Next to this chimney the bunker has a third 'entrance', blown open by the British after their capture of the bunker in September 1917. Of course the Germans knew the exact

German bunkers between the Menin Road and Nonnebossen, 20th September 1917. AWM

Above: a cross-sectional model of the bunker showing the immense thickness of the roof and walls.

No operations took place here, just making the wounded ready for further transport.

operations took place here, just making the wounded ready for further transport. The identification as a German dressing station also explains the extremely wide entrances - up to 2.65 metres.

ARTEFACTS

Due to the use to which it was put after 1940, very few relics were discovered inside the bunker, only a few were found near the British entrance. Two porcelain isolators indicated that the dressing station had electricity. The owner's grandfather, Henri Bauden, confirmed that in the past, electricity and telephone wires had been found in the vicinity of the bunker. The electricity must have been taken from a power station alongside the Menin Road that was originally built to light the 1500 metre long German Hooge Tunnel under the road. An opening through the roof proved to be a small chimney, as the remains of a metal stove were discovered under it. This fell to pieces when

Below: Inside the Cryer Farm complex today.

positions of their own bunkers and in order to prevent shells falling in, the existing entrances were blocked up by the British after capture and a new one was blown through the 1.15 metre thick western wall. The floor is still covered here with two wooden steps. In this southern bunker quite a few pieces of the internal wooden framework are preserved, including the sheet piling of the sump.

With stove and sump, the southernmost block is likely to have been used for logistics. The wounded were collected in the gallery and a doctor could have worked in the first room opposite the main entrance. No

German artefacts found in the vicinity of Cryer Farm. MMP 17

touched and could not be preserved. The third object discovered in the British entrance was a roll of telephone wire marked '1915'.

More artefacts were found on the western side of the bunker; a badly corroded 1915 pattern German steel helmet, six glass bottles, a Prussian 1910 pattern uniform button, an ersatz canteen with cover and leather straps, an enamel mess tin (Bing 1916), a 1916 enamel drinking cup, a 1917 leather gas mask and a 98/05 bayonet with scabbard. Of

'More artefacts were found on the western side of the bunker...'

British origin are a cartridge for a flare pistol, a P 08 buckle and an unmarked Codd bottle. Many German MG bullets, a single and a double 1911 MG ammunition box and parts of a spare barrel for an MG 08 are possibly linked with the Machine Gun that killed Second Lieutenant Cryer as the bullets were all marked pre-1918.

A selection of the retrieved artefacts is on display in the Memorial Museum Passchendaele 1917, together with a scale model of the bunker.

An Australian soldier examining a German bunker between Nonnebossen and Polygon Wood, 20 September 1917. (AWM)

RESTORATION

The first major problem was to clean out the dregs of the former cesspool. In order to solve this a deep pit was made in front of the main entrance in which to drain the waste. From the pit the existing liquid could be pumped away while the sediment was removed by a digging machine. After three days of hard work the bunker was finally cleaned with a pressure washer.

As the floor of the bunker is almost 4 metres underground, a safe entrance had to be made which was built with salvaged German concrete blocks. The post-

> Once inside the construction, everything is left in its original state without any restoration.

1917 blocking of the second entrance was also repaired with original blocks as it is now almost under a farm building. The first and actual main entrance was covered with original German steel sheets like the type used in the original bunker.

Once inside the construction, everything is left in its original state without any restoration. This includes the heavily corroded steel plates and a part of the wooden floor around the sump.

During the restoration we also brought in electricity for a small electrical pump in the historical sump and electric lighting.

93

Luc Bauden, Johan Bostoen, Franky Bostyn and Rik Ryon near the partially opened entrance to Cryer Farm Dressing Station. ABAF

Today the Cryer Farm underground dressing station is the largest surviving bunker so near to the German front line on the former Ypres battlefields. Visiting it is fascinating and will certainly appeal to your imagination. As the bunker is on private property it is only accessible for groups by first contacting the Memorial Museum.

MEMORIAL MUSEUM PASSCHENDAELE 1917

IEPERSTRAAT 5
8980 ZONNEBEKE
BELGIUM

Tel: 0032 51 77 04 41
Fax: 00 32 51 78 07 50

E Mail: info@passchendaele.be
www.zonnebeke.be

SOURCES

Vancoillie, J., Bostyn, F. & Pauwels, M. *Halfweg Menin Road en Ypernstrasse: Gheluvelt 1914-1918* (Voormezele, 2002) passim.

Riess, A. *Das Königlich Bayerische Reserve-Infanterie-Regiment No.4* (Bamberg, 1934) p. 140-142.

Schulz, E. Kissler, A. & Schulze, P. *Geschichte des Reserve-Infanterie-Regiments No. 209 im Weltkriege* (Oldenburg, 1930) p. 171.

Maude, A. *The 47th (London) Division* (London, 1922) p.109.

The National Archives WO 95/2703, 47th Division, September 1917.

Madeleine Sels (Geluveld, Belgium).

Andy Cryer (Marlow, Buckinghamshire).

Special thanks to ABAF vzw, the Community of Zonnebeke, the Luc Bauden-Bogaert family, Johan Bostoen, Rik Ryon and Jürgen Deleye.

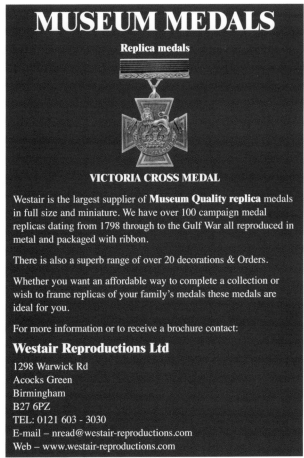

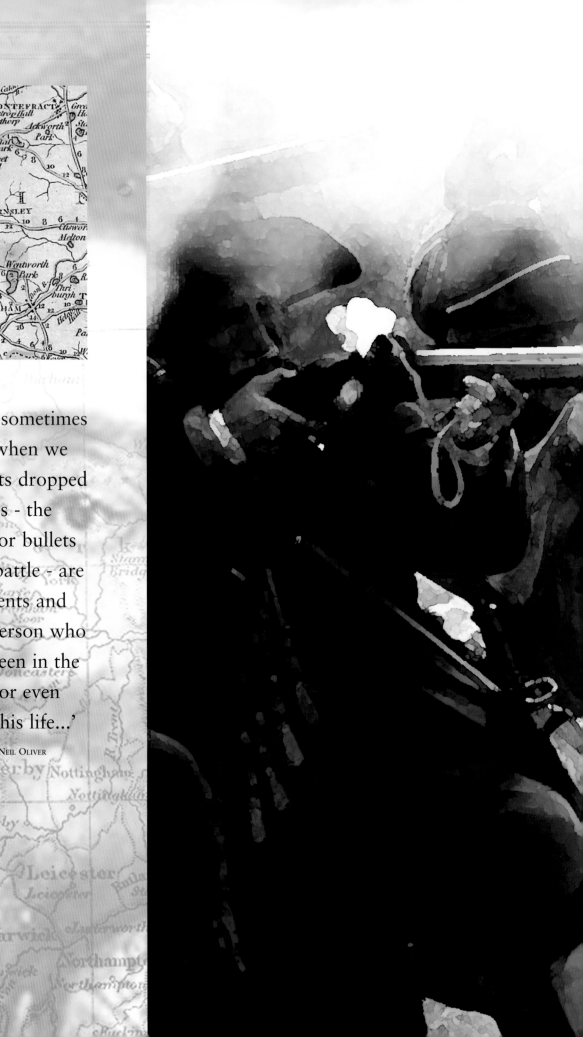

'What we are sometimes looking at when we relocate objects dropped by soldiers - the arrowheads or bullets they used in battle - are the movements and actions of a person who could have been in the last hours or even moments of his life...'

TONY POLLARD & NEIL OLIVER

'MUCH BLOOD HAS BEEN SHED THIS YEAR' - THE BATTLE OF TANKERSLEY MOOR 1643

THE DARTON PARISH REGISTER FOR 1643.

The study of archaeology in general, and battlefield archaeology in particular, is reaching a wider audience through the medium of television. Often, however, the quest for audience figures has necessitated a focus on larger, 'important' battles. But what of the less well-known and obscure battles, skirmishes and encounters and the people caught up in them? Tim Lynch reports from South Yorkshire on one such event.

By Tim Lynch

IN THE LAST DECADE OR SO, the study of archaeology has captured the public imagination as never before. Television has tapped into this with an ever-expanding choice of history and documentary based programming at the forefront of which has been the developing specialism of battlefield archaeology.

Writing about their own television series, Tony Pollard and Neil Oliver admit that their reason for studying battlesites is simple:

'Let's start by being completely honest about why we started studying battlefields in the first place: this stuff can be almost too exciting for words...the experience of doing this type of archaeology is very personal, even intimate. What we are sometimes looking at when we relocate objects dropped by soldiers - the arrowheads or bullets they used in battle, for example - are the movements and actions of a person who could have been in the last hours or even moments of his life...We decided that if archaeology is a way of studying people, then it was about time we found out what archaeological techniques could tell us about war and, more importantly, the people caught up in war.' Welcome though this public interest is, Glenn Foard of the Battlefields Trust has warned that, 'no other events of just a few hours have left such tangible physical remains that can tell us so much of how people interacted with the landscape. However, to yield the answers, the methodology of battlefield investigation needs substantial refinement. This will not be achieved by television, almost the only current source of funding for UK battlefield archaeology!'.

It is said that he who pays the piper calls the tune and to appeal to as wide an audience as possible, television, with its all-important funding, has channelled attention onto the first, last, largest, bloodiest or most famous battles for study. These events, by definition, are exceptional so we should question whether these are really the best medium through which to study the wider experience of any war. Should we focus attention on the interpretation and re-interpretation of those few battles that were so out of the ordinary that they received widespread coverage both then and now or should we seek to study the hundreds of lesser actions that make up the more representative sample? Should we, in other words, pay attention to those actions described by one editor as 'unfortunately not famous enough to be of interest'?

To answer this, we need first to ask ourselves what the

...some archaeologists are, 'troubled by the thought of archaeology as the "handmaiden of history..." '

study of the battlefield is intended to achieve. Foard has remarked that some archaeologists are,

> 'troubled by the thought of archaeology as the "handmaiden of history" and would have a quasi-independent battlefield archaeology. This would be a mistake, for the real opportunity is in uniting military history with historical geography and landscape archaeology. Nor should we be put off by the 'post processual' historians and archaeologists who believed that past soldiers viewed the landscape differently from us, and that battles were more ritual than rational 'modern' interaction with the landscape'.

The aim of battlefield archaeology is to enable us to piece together the story of ordinary people caught up in war and to understand it in terms of the impact it has on their environment. It is an attempt to tell the story of a battle, despite the Duke of Wellington's famous observation that one might as well try to write the history of a dance. For the student of social sciences, though, especially those concerned with the interaction of individuals in small scale, face-to-face communities, there is much to be gained from a study of either. The study of a dance would provide information on the social status, customs, politics and economics of an area, about the aspirations and conflicts among those invited and those who attend. Extending the analogy, archaeology of the dance would tell us about the venue, it might even tell us whether they waltzed, but leaves much to be discovered about why they were dancing there. This then, is the story of one brief action and what it has to tell us of the people involved.

PASSING REFERENCE

In the spring of 1643, royalist forces clashed with their parliamentary foes on a moor on the outskirts of Barnsley in what is now South Yorkshire. The few histories that even acknowledge its existence do so only as a passing reference but, as we shall see, an attempt to examine it in more depth reveals its potential to disclose insights into the context in which it took place. The battle of Tankersley Moor is just one of the hundreds of barely remembered fights across the country in the sporadic but often violent conflicts that erupted throughout the nation during the decade of upheaval variously known as the English Civil War, the Great Rebellion or the Wars of the

Three Kingdoms. Between 1642 and 1652 thousands of homes were destroyed and many thousands of people died as fighting came to towns and villages across the British Isles with an estimated 50,000 royalist and 34,000 parliamentarian soldiers killed in more than 500 known engagements, mostly in the years before 1649. Perhaps another 100,000 died of disease in the same period. With a few highly publicised exceptions, the actions that caused these deaths are anonymous episodes, remembered, if at all, only as local traditions.

Writing in 1992, Philip Tennant argued that,

> 'it is, of course, impossible, after three-and-a-half centuries, to reconstruct a continuous narrative, since although thousands of individuals were caught up in events, few thought to speak or write directly of them, and there is much on which the records remain silent...Nevertheless, one should beware of parish histories which tend to assume that because a village's name is absent from a particular archive the war must have passed it by untouched, for it is unlikely to have been so. There can be little doubt that the contemporary sources...although

'Between 1642 and 1652 thousands of homes were destroyed and many thousands of people died as fighting came to towns and villages across the British Isles'

Brothers at arms. It is estimated that 50,000 royalist and 34,000 parliamentarian troops were killed throughout the wars.

in themselves substantial in quantity, represent the mere tip of a once-considerable iceberg, and that for every single event recorded countless others were not. The testimony of that scholarly eyewitness Richard Baxter is both significant and authoritative: "I think there were very few Parishes where at one time or another Blood has not been shed".'

THE BACKGROUND

The Yorkshire campaign of 1643 has been widely discussed elsewhere [(see, for example, David Cooke's *The Civil War in Yorkshire* (Pen & Sword, 2004), or Peter Newman's *Royalist Army in the North* (York PhD Thesis 1978)] and we need only a brief description here.

Locations of garrisons and forges in area of battlefield.

> **"I think there were very few Parishes where at one time or another Blood has not been shed".'**

In January 1642, after years of increasing bitterness between the king and parliament, Charles I headed north to York to set up a military base independent of parliamentary restraint. It was the culmination of a decade in which Charles had refused to allow parliament to encroach on what he saw as his divine right to rule absolutely. In 1639, he had brought the country to the brink of war with Scotland, and only last minute negotiations prevented any real fighting. Another brief war the following year saw Charles lead his English army in defeat at Newburn but he broke the royal finances in doing so. When, shortly after the English army had been demobilised from this second war, rebellion broke out in Ireland, Charles reluctantly turned to parliamentary revenue to fund a new military expedition. Parliament was concerned that a well-equipped army under the command of the king could be used against them if he were truly determined to exercise absolutist power. Rebellion against the king at this time was unthinkable but parliamentary members determined to restrain the king by removing the support of his 'evil counsellors'. Chief amongst these dangerous men was Thomas Wentworth, the Earl of Stafford, a Yorkshireman from Wentworth Woodhouse in South Yorkshire who enjoyed popular support among the local gentry. His impeachment and trial for treason, orchestrated by enemies within parliament, culminated in his execution in 1641 and drove the wedge between the king and parliament that would lead to war.

As he moved north, the king became locked in a struggle with parliament for control of the local militia. Parliament had used the Militia Ordinance to confuse the issue so instead, at his northern stronghold in York, Charles re-introduced the medieval Commission of Array. First introduced in 1327 and used last in 1557, the commission was intended to counter foreign invasion and gave the commissioners, empowered by the king, the authority to call up all able bodied men for military service. Those unfit to serve were required to contribute to the upkeep of the army through taxation. The noted historian Peter Newman tells us that, *'the first specifically military development in the north, predating the commission of May 11th, seems to have come from a local justice of the peace, Sir Francis Wortley. According to a report, he unambiguously drew his sword on May 3rd and publicly declared for the king, and by the 12th was recruiting 200 gentlemen to form a Royal Lifeguard of Horse. A Trained Band infantry regiment was also brought in as a Lifeguard, that of Sir Robert Strickland'.*

Wortley, a close friend and near neighbour of Thomas Wentworth, is central to the story that follows.

In February 1642, Charles' catholic wife, Henrietta Maria, had been sent to Holland to procure weapons and military experts. To facilitate her return, Charles intended to seize the arsenal at Hull and to use the port as his supply base. His failure to secure Hull after several attempts meant that instead he was forced to turn to the ports further up the north east coast and called upon William Cavendish, the Earl of Newcastle to secure these for him. Initially, Newcastle's role was simply to provide a safe landing place for Henrietta Maria and the supplies she would bring but by July 1642, Charles had conferred on him the Generalship of all Royalist forces north of the Trent and gave him wide powers to raise troops, grant commissions and even knighthoods. After securing agreements about the funding of his force, Newcastle crossed into Yorkshire to secure the county for the king.

There followed a campaign that saw Newcastle's forces push the parliamentary forces, under the command of Ferdinando and Thomas Fairfax, back into pockets of fierce resistance amongst the mill towns of West Yorkshire but throughout, Newcastle's priority remained that of ensuring the safe passage of the queen and her supplies to the king's army at Oxford. Newcastle has been criticised for his failure to follow through his early successes but the arrival of Henrietta Maria at York in March 1643 diverted his attention away from securing the defeat of the Fairfaxes and towards the defence of York in order to prepare the way south. The first convoy of 1,500 men and weapons left the city in April 1643. The chain of events that led to Tankersley Moor had been set in motion.

Writing about this period, Hilaire Belloc commented that,

'the numbers engaged upon either side of the struggle were usually small. Skirmishes outside

> 'Skirmishes outside country houses are dignified by the name of sieges; a mêlée of a few horse is often called a battle... '

country houses are dignified by the name of sieges; a mêlée of a few horse is often called a battle, while the lack of plan and purpose in much of the fighting makes the general observer underrate, if anything, the position of this English episode in the general military history of the seventeenth century'.

Before embarking on a search for the battle of Tankersley Moor, or indeed any battle of this period, we need, considering Belloc's comments, firstly to establish whether there actually is a battle to seek. If, as he suggests, 'actions' of this period may be little more than one group of youths with bad hairstyles indulging in a slanging match with their floppy-hatted neighbours, what evidence do we have that a significant fight took place?

LOCAL EVIDENCE

Local tradition of the Tankersley area, gleaned from a variety of sources, tells us that Sir Francis Wortley of nearby Wortley Hall was an ardent royalist who raised a force of 900 men from his estate to fight the parliamentary army on the moor in 1647. During the battle, Tankersley Hall was destroyed and Sir Francis taken prisoner. He died in the Tower of London some years later. A cart at Wortley Forge industrial museum is said to have been used by his forces at Tankersley and at Marston Moor. Unfortunately, as so often with local tradition, there are a few errors: he didn't, it wasn't, he wasn't and the date is wrong! The cart, fully original except for the replaced wheels and extensive refurbishment of the body, is first recorded as having been used in 1647, four years after Tankersley and three years after Marston Moor. Nevertheless, we have a starting point.

More detailed local histories are equally frustrating. Writing a history of nearby Worsbrough in 1872, Joseph Wilkinson referred to a local man, Mr Bashforth, who *'could relate no small amount of traditionary lore touching the exploits of Cromwell and his army at Houndhill, Stainborough, Tankersley, and the surrounding villages'.* Unfortunately, he does not appear to have considered any of this lore worth recording. A few years later, in 1876, the first recorded physical evidence surfaced, when an ash tree near the church was cut down and a 'musket ball' found. (The description given is of a bullet, one and a half inches long, hollow for half its length which suggests that it may, in fact, be the cap of a powder flask. Unfortunately, the item has since disappeared). Then, in 1917, cannon balls were

Case containing cannonballs and early 18th century map of Tankersley Park in St Peter's Church, Tankersley.

discovered along Tankersley Lane. Clearly then, a fight of some sort had taken place here.

Although the story is known locally, no serious research into the battle appears to have been undertaken. An Internet search revealed just two accounts of the battle, one by Simon Wright, who portrays one of Newcastle's Whitecoats as a member of the Sealed Knot re-enactment society and the other, heavily based on Mr Wright's account, by wargamer Noel Williams. Neither makes any claim to be an historian and so the material is not intended as anything other than an attempt to open discussion about the battle but Mr Wright does at least point the way.

THE DOCUMENTARY EVIDENCE

The only direct contemporary source we have for the battle comes from the Duchess of Newcastle's memoirs of her husband. At the end of March 1643, the royalists had routed the enemy at Seacroft Moor near Leeds and had taken about 800 prisoners.

'Immediately after, in pursuit of that victory, my lord sent a considerable party into the West of Yorkshire, where they met with about 2,000 of the enemy's forces, taken out of their several garrisons in those parts to execute some design upon a moor called Tankersley Moor, and there fought them, and routed them; many were slain, and some taken prisoners.'

This would appear to place the battle in early April. However, the Duchess would seem to have made a slight error in her chronology. In the immediate aftermath of Seacroft Moor, Newcastle advanced against Leeds with the intention of taking the town but, after a short bombardment, deferred to his deputy, James King, and instead shifted his attention to the capture and consolidation of nearby Wakefield.

Once the garrison was established, the Duchess reports that,

'receiving intelligence that in two market towns southwest from Wakefield viz Rotherham and Sheffield, the enemie was very busie to raise forces against his majesty and had fortified them both about four miles distant from each other hoping thereby to give protection and encouragement to all those parts of the country which were populous rich and rebellious, he thought it necessary to use his best endeavours in April 1643 to march with part of his army from Wakefield into the mentioned parts, attended with a train of artillery and ammunition, leaving the greatest part of it in Wakefield'.

Newcastle's men began to advance south towards their targets and royalist forces took control of Barnsley, roughly halfway between Wakefield and Rotherham. On 20th April, Sir Thomas Fairfax reported to his father that,

'some of the Penistone men came also to demand aid, there being seventeen colours in Barnsley, five miles of them. I advised them to seek help from Rotherham and Sheffield, and whilst they stood upon their guards to get their goods to places of most safeguard, for it will be impossible without more horse to defend the county from spoil'.

Waiting for Newcastle's men at Barnsley were infantry,

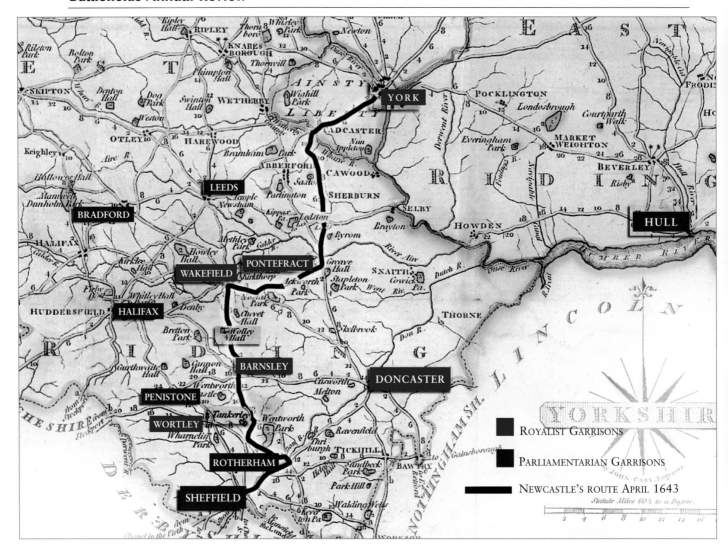

dragoons and horse raised by Wortley and other local gentry and currently garrisoned at his own house and nearby Tankersley Hall.

Fairfax's advice to the parliamentary garrison at Penistone seems to have been heeded and the royalist news sheet *Mercurius Aulicus*, in a report dated 6th May 1643, describes how;

> 'the Earle of Newcastle's forces in the North encountered...with a body of the Rebels, consisting of 3000 men (which were going, as it is conceived, to the relief of Leeds) & had so fortunate success therein, that they totally routed the whole body of them, 150 of them being killed in the place, 240 prisoners taken'.

From this we can tentatively date the battle in the last week or so of April with corroborating evidence for the date coming from an entry in the Barnsley Parish

'...they totally routed the whole body of them, 150 of them being killed in the place, 240 prisoners taken'.

Registers dated 1st May 1643 which records the burial of 'Luke Carleil, Willm Dobson, Luke Garfield, soldiers', several days before the next known action in the area, the attack on Rotherham on 4th May. In nearby Sheffield, the burials of three men, one identified only as 'a souglier', are recorded as having taken place on 6th May, a date two days before the attack on Sheffield began and it is possible that these men, too, were casualties of the battle.

THE CONTEXT

By late April, the royalist army in the north had forced a wedge across Yorkshire from the northeast to the southwest of the county. York, Pontefract, Wakefield and Doncaster were all in Newcastle's hands. In Hull, Sir John Hotham was seriously reconsidering his decision to hold the port for parliament. In the West Riding mill towns of Leeds, Bradford, Halifax and Huddersfield, the

Fairfaxes were besieged and rapidly running out of resources to reinforce outlying districts such as the garrison of Penistone at the southern extremity of this enclave. To the south, Rotherham and Sheffield Castle were both held by Parliament and threatened the safety of any convoy travelling beyond the county. These latter garrisons could be reinforced from Nottinghamshire and Derbyshire respectively and, as Newcastle's men advanced on Rotherham, the Parliamentary commander in Derbyshire, Sir John Gell, was assembling a force equipped with cannon to do just that. Further afield, Cromwell was drawing up plans for a relief column to be sent to support the Fairfaxes. The plan was abandoned after Hotham's son, now committed to changing sides, wrote to assure Cromwell that the force was no longer needed.

Across the Pennines in Lancashire, the hundreds of Blackburn and Salford had declared for parliament from the outset. These towns bordered on the parliamentary enclaves in Yorkshire and the old Roman roads that led across the moors to Bradford, Penistone and Sheffield made them an obvious choice to supply reinforcements. Fairfax had expected the arrival of troops from Lancashire by April 20th and by the time of the Adwalton Moor battle, 1600 troops had joined him from across the border. In southwest Yorkshire, the only thing standing between the southern forces and the West Riding towns was the garrison established by Sir Francis Wortley at Tankersley and in his own home, Wortley Hall. Against this background, the order from Fairfax to the Penistone garrison and the report in *Mercurius Aulicus* both support the theory that a force, probably from Rotherham, was advancing to break through to Penistone in order to link up the two armies.

In addition to the linking of the forces, such an attack could have another important aim. Tankersley sits atop a seam of ironstone and since the 13th century this had been mined to feed the local iron industry. The Wortley family's fortunes were closely tied to ironworking, owning as they did forges in the Wharncliffe valley, at Wortley itself and as far north as Halifax. Within a few miles of Tankersley, major forges were in operation at Kimberworth, Wadsley and Wortley Top and all are known to have been involved in

weapons manufacture during this period. Capturing or destroying these could seriously impede the ammunition starved royalist army's advance or at least hamper the expected siege of Sheffield Castle.

Finally, the destruction of the Wortley garrison and the family's business interests would have been of great personal satisfaction to Sir John Gell, who had secured Sheffield Castle in October 1642 and who commanded forces in neighbouring Derbyshire. Gell had clashed with Sir Francis Wortley's troopers several times during their incursions into his territory throughout that autumn.

THE ROYALIST FORCES

We do not know the exact size or composition of the force that left Wakefield but the Fairfax letter states 'seventeen colours' in Barnsley by late April. If these were infantry, it would indicate a force of 1500 and perhaps as high as 2000 men. Even if these were smaller units of horse, it would still represent a sizeable force, growing as local garrisons and trained bands appear to have linked up with the force.

At the core, though, two regiments seem to be prime candidates for forming the convoy. Sir William Savile of Thornhill, near Wakefield, had had close ties with the Earl of Stafford and had now established a regiment from his estates across the region. Savile, later appointed Governor of Sheffield Castle, was of a family which had historic links with the Tankersley area and would therefore be a logical choice of commander. Peter Newman's analysis of the Northern

> 'Rotherham and Sheffield Castle were both held by Parliament and threatened the safety of any convoy travelling beyond the county.'

Army places Colonel George Wentworth's Regiment of Foot in Wakefield and this could also make them a sensible choice. Wentworth, a kinsman of Thomas Wentworth, was from the Woolley area, approximately a third of the distance between the garrison at Wakefield and Tankersley and so would know the area and people well.

Newman cites a muster roll found in the Wentworth family archives which describes 71 men in three 'rankes'. This, he argues, would normally be suggestive of a cavalry unit and asks whether the roll may relate to either Savile's regiment or a pre-war trained band muster. The presence of John Oxley, Thomas English, Nicholas Burkley and Henry Carrington in the list of the 'third ranke' is noted in a 1907 history of Barnsley, supporting the view that these men were prominent local citizens of the Militia. In any case, if these men were in Yorkshire, their local knowledge and connections would make them the obvious choice to lead the attack.

Of the troops and commanders available to Newcastle, only Sir Francis Wortley and his dragoons, are known with any certainty to have been part of the force. Wortley, as we have seen, was the first to raise forces for the king when he established a unit of 200 horse to act as the king's lifeguard. This force went with the royalist army to Hull and seems to have made something of a nuisance of itself, earning a special mention in Hotham's report to parliament. From here, it may be that Wortley took part in the Edgehill campaign. Certainly we can place his force in Warwickshire in October 1642 and in November of that year Wortley was implicated in complaints of plunder from Shropshire, Staffordshire, Cheshire and Derbyshire as his men headed home from the campaign.

Returning home, he fortified his own Wortley Hall and the nearby Tankersley Hall and a warrant dated late in 1642 tells us:

> 'Whereas, on the establishment of the garrison commanded by Sir Francis Wortley, knight and baronet, at Tankersley or thereabouts, agreed upon the two and twentieth day of July last past, and subscribed by his Excellencie the Earl of Newcastle, the several parishes enumerated are appointed to pay to the said Sir Francis Wortley, for the mainteynance of his said garrison (which is to consist of one hundred and fiftie dragoons besides officers) the sum of eighty-five pounds fifteen shillings five pence farthinge by the weeke'.

At first inspection Sir Francis, like many of his contemporaries, appears to have been remarkably long lived and robust until closer examination of the family tree reveals that care needs to be taken when examining records based solely on the name of the individual. The Francis Wortley who attended Mary Queen of Scots during her long imprisonment at Sheffield is not the same one as the man who drew his sword at York or who bequeathed his estate to his illegitimate daughter in 1668. In fact, Sir Francis was the grandson of Francis Wortley and was created baronet in 1611, at the age of 19. His son, also named Sir Francis, is described by Martyn Bennett as having been a cavalry commander under Henry Hastings and so we can begin to make some separation between the 50 year old local commander and his 22 year old cavalry officer son. From the sources available, it would seem to have been the elder man who fought at Tankersley Moor.

Having established garrisons at Tankersley and Wortley, Sir Francis enthusiastically set about raising taxes and assessments against the local population, ranging so far afield that he drew complaints from the commander of the royalist garrison at Pontefract Castle. The Puritan diarist, Oliver Heywood writes of Wortley having 'roved up and down the country robbing and taxing many honest people'. Spencer writes of him as;

> 'the most troublesome in the district for besides being a thorn in the flesh of the local parliamentary forces, he levied lays and assessments on both friend and foe alike'.

Somewhat confusingly, Wortley appears in the lists of Royalist officers as having commanded horse, dragoon and foot units. We have seen that he raised a unit of horse at the outbreak of war and garrisoned his local commands with dragoons. His attempts to raise infantry were somewhat less successful as a set of orders indicates. Having decided that he would have difficulty in raising a full regiment, Wortley ordered the constables to round up 500 men. Even this number proved elusive, much to his embarrassment. The policy of *posse comitatus* rendered every man between 16 and 60 eligible for service in case of invasion. Few men conscripted for local defence were willing to leave their homes and livelihoods for an unspecified length of time to serve outside their own home districts. Nevertheless,

'Having established garrisons at Tankersley and Wortley, Sir Francis enthusiastically set about raising taxes and assessments against the local population'.

Wortley appears to have been almost a stereotypically dashing, enthusiastic and committed cavalier commander in this crucial stage of the war.

PARLIAMENTARY FORCES.

If we know little about the royalist force, we know even less about the parliamentary troops facing them. In October 1642, Sir John Gell had taken Sheffield Castle for Parliament and set John Bright to work recruiting for the garrison. Things do not appear to have gone well and by September 1642, a report talks of Gell being, *'importuned to help there at Sheaffield to suppress a mutiny there'* (although another source shifts this to a place called Wheatfield). We do know, however, that Sheffield was later surrendered without resistance, thus calling into question the ability of the garrison to send out an aggressive force.

Rotherham, by contrast, appears to have taken its support of parliament seriously. When the royalist army approached the town along the road from Tankersley, it found the way blocked by a barricade manned by 30 boys from the local grammar school. Accounts then differ. The royalists claim that the town fell in one day, their opponents claim that it took at least two days to quell resistance. Whatever the case, some '1400 armes' were found indicating that the town could have been well defended.

It seems likely, then, that the force advancing north towards the West Riding at Tankersley was from Rotherham. No parliamentary account of the action has yet been found so we have only the two royalist estimates of the number of troops as something between 2-3000. Assuming at least some level of

exaggeration for propaganda purposes, it would be reasonable to believe that the forces were relatively evenly matched in terms of numbers.

'Sir John Gell had taken Sheffield Castle for Parliament and set John Bright to work recruiting for the garrison.'

THE BATTLEFIELD

At Seacroft and Adwalton Moor, manoeuvring armies had met and clashed on the march across the terrain they happened to be in. Tankersley Moor, however, would seem to have been a more planned engagement. The Moor was a site well known to many on both sides and records show that it and neighbouring Harley Moor were used several times as training areas by local trained bands in the years leading up to the war.

The area itself sits in a shallow saddle between hilly country on both sides. It forms a gently sloping but relatively even expanse of land immediately to the south of what is now Junction 36 of the M1 motorway. Although much of the adjacent land has been drastically altered by the building of roads, a golf course and the encroachment of housing developments, there is still a large and relatively undisturbed area into which a battle of the scale suggested by the Duchess of Newcastle could fit.

According to an unpublished account of the battle held in the local library, *'the Royalist army came on by Moor Lane'*. The author does not give any provenance for this information, but it appears logical. If the royalist army were in Barnsley, they would advance via the village of Worsbrough to the Moor along what is now the A61 (the current route bypassing the village was established as a turnpike in 1840). It is worth noting that the A6135, which acts as a continuation south to Rotherham, is also known as Wakefield Road and this would be the most likely route

> 'The Moor was a site well known to many on both sides...'

for the advancing parliamentary force. This is corroborated by accounts of the royalist assault on Rotherham having advanced through Masbrough along this road. Both sides would therefore have marched parallel to the present day line of the M1 on its eastern side.

The site of the moor has been identified by reference to local place names. A short path just north of the motorway junction is known as 'Moor Lane', and leads now to a footbridge across the motorway into Tankersley. This position was

View South from Tankersley Lane (site of the cannonball finds). St Peter's Church is in the trees to the right.

ST PETER'S CHURCH

View north from Tankersley Lane. (On the left of the shot is a white line – this marks Moor Lane – the traditional start line for the Royalists.)

confirmed on an 1855 Ordnance Survey map which identified 'Moor Lane' as continuing in the direction indicated by the footbridge, linking into the A61 route today. A couple of hundred metres away is a large hotel, now known as Tankersley Manor but in 1855 identified as 'Moor Farm'. The area south of Moor Lane is designated 'Tankersley Common' and it is safe to assume that this is the moor itself. Today, the common exists as a patch of land adjacent to the motorway junction.

Taking Moor Lane as our start line, the battlefield may be the area from here, south across Tankersley Lane where the cannonballs were discovered in 1917. These cannon balls appear to be of a variety of calibres and were probably used at fairly close range. Wargamer Noel Williams suggests that the slight ridge made by Tinker Hill and the commanding site of St Peter's Church would make this a good defensive position, although this would shift the parliamentary forces away from the road link with their rear. They would effectively have wooded hillsides to their rear and right flank and royalists to their front and left flank.

Some sources place the fighting in and around Tankersley Hall but this seems unlikely since the hall stood in the midst of an established deer park. The park, owned by Lord Stafford, is recorded as being in existence by 1527 and a herd of deer remained in the park as late as 1850. Melvyn Jones has described the creation of deer parks as involving;

> '*enclosing an area of land with a fence to keep the deer and other game in, and predators (wolves) and poachers out. The fence was called the park pale and consisted of either cleft oak*

St Peter's Church. Fighting is believed to have taken place around here.

View from St Peter's north over Tankersley Moor.

stakes, often set on a bank, or a stone wall. Tankersley Park, one of the longest surviving local medieval parks, was completely surrounded by a stone wall'.

Whether the wall existed to that extent at the time of the battle is unclear but a map of 1720 shows it in place. Within the walls, the park consisted of dense woodland and plains with scattered trees, coppice and 'holly hags' - areas of holly bushes grown as winter fodder. The park would be a difficult place to manoeuvre troops so we can identify this as the southern boundary of our battlefield.

'...much elated the enemy and cast down the spirits of the people of these parts...'

OUTCOME

Shortly after the battle, royalist troops took Rotherham. Accounts differ with the royalists claiming that it fell in one day, Parliamentarians making much of the scratch defence put up by thirty boys from the local grammar school and claiming that it held for two days against a much larger force. Days later, Sheffield Castle fell with minimal resistance. Tankersley Moor is described as having been a rout and it would appear that the news was enough to thoroughly demoralise the parliamentary garrisons. Fairfax was to write that the loss of the garrisons,

Various types of cannonballs found in the Tankersley area.

'...much elated the enemy and cast down the spirits of the people of these parts...The Earl of Newcastle's Army do now range over all the Southwest part of the Countrey, pillaging and cruelly using the well affected party'.

The capture of Sheffield Castle was of great value to the supply starved royalists. It was to become a munitions factory supplying weapons and ammunition to Pontefract for dispersal. The forge at Wortley was certainly part of this effort and cannonballs from the period have been unearthed there.

As well as opening the route south, the fight ensured that the Fairfaxes were alone and under pressure. It was to be a significant contribution to the eventual royalist control of Yorkshire.

CONCLUSION

Set against the wider conflict, the campaign in southwest Yorkshire has been just a footnote in the history of the Civil Wars but just because it is not famous, does that make it uninteresting? What can an archaeological survey of Tankersley tell us?

Tankersley was not a large or unusual battle. That is the key to its importance. We have here the opportunity to investigate a site that was selected by men who knew it as a training area. It is as if Salisbury Plain were selected to be the site of a major battle fought by men who had learned their craft there. It should, therefore, be almost a textbook example of how to fight such an action. It is hoped that a metal detector survey can be carried out in order to track the action and perhaps identify the deployment of forces.

It also offers us the chance to strengthen the links between battlefield archaeology and landscape work. The Ordnance Survey maps show the presence of a moat at the end of Tankersley Lane, probably the site of the first fortified building here in 900AD. Medieval mineworkings and ironworks surround the site and the deer park can still be traced. It is a concentration of evidence of man's impact on his environment - that in itself is worthy of investigation.

More importantly, perhaps, we need to remember that no battle takes place in a vacuum. Returning to our dance analogy, fieldwork will reveal the venue, the type of dance and maybe even some of the partygoers, but there is much more to learn. To draw from the field of psychology, a battle is a gestalt entity. It is only understood as the sum of its parts and we need to look for patterns of thinking and behaviour that make up that sum. Peter Harrington has argued that more work 'needs to be focussed upon the role of country houses in their role as garrisoned strongholds during the war' and Tankersley allows us to do just that. Sir Francis Wortley raised a garrison for two adjoining country houses and

109

used them as bases from which to stamp his authority on the surrounding areas. The early days of the Civil War were as much about economics as military might and, perhaps labouring our dance analogy now, we need to look carefully at those who chose not to go to the ball.

History tends to tell us that Yorkshire was predominantly royalist and, to an extent, this is true. However, as JT Cliffe has shown in his analysis of the Yorkshire gentry, this is not the whole story. In the West Riding of Yorkshire, the area that encompasses both the mill towns and the Rotherham/Sheffield region, he notes that 125 families declared for the king whilst only 54 were for parliament. Significantly, though, 110 families remained neutral. The activities of Wortley and his men become important here in levying taxes but also in demonstrating to those neutralist families that parliament could not protect them. It would be useful to see how this fear might have influenced the 31 families whose loyalties switched during the course of the war and the impact of this economic war on the local economy. By the time of the defeat of Fairfax at Adwalton Moor, he was to declare that West Yorkshire had been bled dry.

Battlefield archaeology is about the study of ordinary people in war. Even a historically insignificant event has much to tell us. Physical evidence will tell us a great deal. Historical evidence will add to the picture. Experimental archaeology will fill in the technical gaps. We can develop a sophisticated narrative for almost any event,

but if we are to understand the gestalt, we need to consider not only why so many fought to the end so loyally for the king that they lost their homes, their fortunes and their lives, but perhaps to ask why so many others didn't.

Sadly, however, whatever lessons Tankersley has to offer, the chance to learn is limited. Tim Sutherland of the Conflict Archaeology International Research Network has argued that on any battlefield, the topsoil layer is vital. It is here that most artefacts will be found and Tankersley, it appears - because it has not been subject to extensive ploughing - could be virtually intact. Economically, though, what lies below Tankersley has value and the area is soon to be destroyed to make way for open cast mining. If seemingly 'famous' battlesites often appear to have little legal protection, then what of the future for sites like Tankersley? Are they soon to be lost forever?

SELECT BIBLIOGRAPHY

Glenn Foard, Field Offensive *British Archaeology*, Issue 79, November 2004.

Peter Harrington, *English Civil War Archaeology* (English Heritage/BT Batsford Books: 2004).

Melvyn Jones, *The Making of the South Yorkshire Landscape*, (Wharncliffe Books: 2000).

Tony Pollard & Neil Oliver *Two Men in a Trench*, Michael Joseph Books (2002).

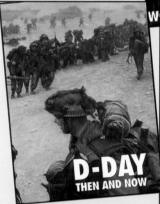

'The conflict between nobles and Cossacks would periodically boil over into outright Cossack revolt and rebellion, most of which were crushed without much mercy.'

FIGHTING FOR FREEDOM: THE 1649 WAR BETWEEN THE COSSACKS AND THE POLISH-LITHUANIAN COMMONWEALTH

To most westerners, the Cossacks remain a mysterious and romanticized people. Nineteenth century writers and artists depict the Cossacks as extraordinary horsemen. This image is often reinforced by descriptions of Cossacks immune to the vigour of the Russian winter as they continued to nip at the heels of Napoleon's Grand Army in 1812. Novels, like Gogol's *Taras Bulba*, and the opera *Mazepa*, suggest the Cossacks were both cruel and crafty, while others highlight their barbarity and backwardness.

By Dr Adrian Mandzy

SUCH STEREOTYPES ARE OF LIMITED VALUE, the term Cossack has evolved over time. Initially the term was used as a verb to indicate a specific part-time activity that men undertook when in the 'unsettled' or 'wild lands' of the steppe. In the sixteenth, seventeenth, and eighteenth centuries, the Cossacks lived in independent communities along the frontiers of Muscovy, the Polish-Lithuanian Commonwealth, and the Ottoman Empire. Like the *courier-de-bois* and cowboys of the Americas, Cossacks hunted, fished, traded, and explored sparsely settled regions. Periodically, males journeyed to the open frontier, spent their time 'cossacking' and returned home. Others joined the Cossacks and spent their lives raiding settlements in search of loot.

Throughout the sixteenth century, as magnates began to place ever-increasing restrictions on peasants and subjugate them to ever-increasing servitude, many villagers fled to the steppe frontier. Not all Cossacks, however, were previously farmers - nobles, burghers and former priests could also be found amongst this social estate. Over

Nineteenth century artistic depiction of a Cossack Officer.

time, as these social outcasts became ever more skilled in the military arts, Cossack year-round fortified camps developed. Royal officials of the Commonwealth, fearful of the growing number of armed Cossacks, began recruiting these freemen as border guards. So successful were the Cossacks in their military abilities that by the end of the sixteenth century foreign governments appealed to the Cossacks for aid.

Since the Cossacks saw themselves as defenders of the frontiers, they believed that they had the same rights and privileges as the nobles who defended the realm. In times of war monarchs reaffirmed Cossack privileges and in times of peace, nobles sought to limit Cossack authority. The conflict between nobles and Cossacks would periodically boil over into outright Cossack revolt and rebellion, most of which were crushed without much mercy. Yet of all the Cossack wars for rights and freedom, Bohdan Khmelnytsky's successful war against the Polish-Lithuanian Commonwealth changed the face of Europe forever.

Bohdan Zenovij Khmelnytsky (c. 1595-

General map of Central Europe showing the locations of the battlefield.

A 1651 engraving of the Ukrainian Cossack leader, Hetman Bohdan Khmelnytsky.

1657) was born on his father's estate at Subotiv, in what is today Central Ukraine. After completing his education, Bohdan joined his father in a war against the Ottoman Turks and in 1620 he was captured following the battle of Cecora (Moldavia). After two years of captivity in Istanbul, Khmelnytsky's ransom was paid and he returned home to his estate at Subotiv. In time, he rose to the rank of colonel, but in 1638, based on a rumour of his participation in a failed Cossack rebellion he was demoted to captain. Over the next decade, Khmelnytsky offered his services to the monarchy and was involved in the development of his estate. In 1646, a raid by a Polish nobleman on Khmelnytsky's property resulted in the death of his youngest son. Khmelnytsky tried to find redress to his claims in the courts of the Polish-Lithuanian Commonwealth, which then ruled Ukraine. While the modern day Polish state considers itself to be the direct

successor of the Polish-Lithuanian Commonwealth, it was in fact a multi-ethnic and multi-religious state in which class was more important than nationality or religion. During the mid-seventeenth century, many old established Ukrainian nobles held key offices within the Polish-Lithuanian Commonwealth.

As a Cossack, Khmelnytsky could not attain justice in a legal system controlled by nobles and in the autumn of 1647, he was placed under arrest on the orders of the local magistrate. After escaping custody, in January 1648, Khmelnytsky fled to the Zaporozhian Sich, the Cossack armed camp located south of the Dnipro River rapids.[1] Now beyond the reach of Polish authorities, Khmelnytsky persuaded the local Cossacks that they needed to defend their rights and rebel against their injustices. Unlike other previous Cossack rebellions, which failed due to the lack of cavalry,[2] Khmelnytsky created an alliance with the Muslim Crimean Tatars.

Together, these two traditional enemies faced the largest and one of the most powerful states in Europe - the Polish-Lithuanian Commonwealth.

In May 1648, Hetman[3] Khmelnytsky defeated two Polish-Lithuanian armies, one at Zhovti Vody and another at Korsun. Ukrainian regiments, who served in the Polish-Lithuanian armies, defected to Khmelnytsky's banner. Invigorated by the success of the Cossacks, serfs, peasants and urban dwellers also rebelled. In this 'Great Revolt', Jews, Catholics and Polish nobles were killed or driven out from what is today Central Ukraine. Polish nobles responded to the massacres in kind and employed their own terror tactics. Following the destruction of a third Polish-Lithuanian army at Pyliavtsi, Khmelnytsky returned to Kiev where the Ukrainian Orthodox hierarchy treated him as a liberator.

Yet in spite of these dramatic victories, the relationship between the rebellious Ukrainians and the Commonwealth remained unclear. The Cossack elite and long-serving rank and file had fought to secure the rights and privileges of noblemen. Others within the Orthodox hierarchy fought for parity with Catholics. Serfs, peasants and the lower urban classes struggled against economic exploitation. Since neither Khmelnytsky nor the monarch could propose a peaceful solution to the ongoing conflict, the war continued into 1649.

In preparation for the spring campaign, more Cossacks, peasants, townsmen, and nobles joined Khmelnytsky and his Tatar ally Khan Islam Girei. Against this force stood three separate Polish armies and a Lithuanian army. The Polish armies struck first and consolidated their forces at the fortress of Zbarazh under Prince Jeremi Wisniowiecki, while the Lithuanian army moved south to attack Khmelnytsky's forces. In such a manner, the Commonwealth hoped to trap Khmelnytsky between the Polish and the Lithuanian army. Unfortunately for the Commonwealth, the Cossacks were able to turn back the Lithuanian army and advance on the Polish army at Zbarazh. On 29 June, Khmelnytsky reached Zbarazh and besieged the Polish army. Surrounded and outnumbered, the only hope of salvation lay in the timely arrival of a relief force.

The newly elected King Jan Casimir, personally led a second army to free the Polish troops trapped at Zbarazh. Leaving a force behind to maintain the siege, Khmelnytsky moved to intercept the king. Outside the

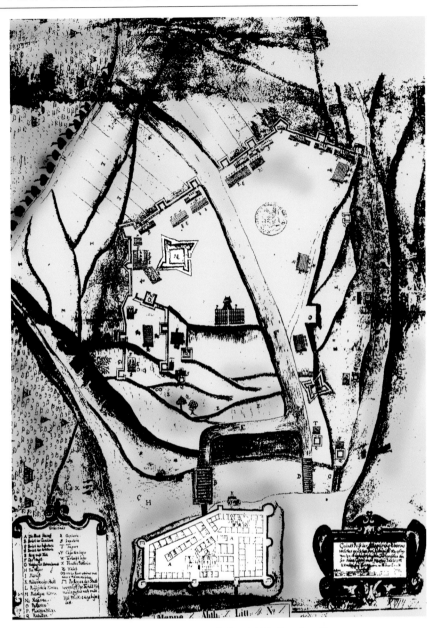

A 1649 military engineering map of the 1649 Battle of Zboriv; most likely completed by Christopher Houwaldt, a Saxon. The original map is in Berlin.

town of Zboriv, less than a day's ride from Zbarazh, Khmelnytsky ambushed the monarch's army as it crossed the Strypa River. Suffering heavy losses, the Polish-Lithuanian forces established a defensive perimeter and as evening fell, the king's army constructed earthworks in preparation for the coming battle. In the morning, Cossacks and Tatars breached the partially completed defensive works. German troops in the service of the crown successfully counter-attacked and sealed the breaches in the line, but in doing so the king exhausted his only remaining military reserves. Surrounded and with no hope for rescue, the crown

The newly elected Polish King, Jan Casimir.

opened negotiations with the rebels. The resulting Treaty of Zboriv created an autonomous Ukrainian Cossack state.[4]

Not surprisingly, the Wars of Bohdan Khmelnytsky are among the most important events in the history of East Central Europe. Over the last few centuries, Ukrainian, Polish and Jewish scholars have devoted a great deal of time and energy in the pursuit of this topic and the documentary evidence was thoroughly examined. While new discoveries are periodically made in the archives of Western Europe and Turkey, those in Central and East Europe have been well studied since the end of the nineteenth century. Thus, while perceptions of Khmelnytsky and the Cossack Wars periodically undergo change, these interpretations rely almost exclusively on the same body of knowledge.

With the development of battlefield studies and battlefield archaeology, it is possible to provide a new perspective of people who are poorly represented within the documentary record. This applies to non-literate societies who left no historic record, those ignored in the historical record (the poor, illiterate or marginalised groups), and those whose documents were destroyed. As the Cossacks were both a group that developed on Europe's eastern fringes and whose records were later deliberately destroyed by order of the Russian monarchy, to learn more about the Cossacks and their wars, we need to go beyond just the diplomatic history of the Cossack elite. We need to look at the material culture of the Cossacks to understand more about the people who lived on Europe's eastern frontier.

Although scholars have provided differing interpretations of the events at Zboriv and Zbarazh, little work has been previously attempted to incorporate the local topography, historical accounts and the

Late twentieth century artistic depiction of the 1st day's fighting at the Battle of Zboriv. Mural on display at the Zboriv Regional Museum.

archaeological record into a holistic interpretation of these events.[5] The first attempt to link the historical accounts of the battlefield with the local topography was undertaken by the Ukrainian historian Ivan Krypiakevych, who created a series of maps of the battle based on his two-day visit to Zboriv in July of 1929.[6] The Soviet regime made a concerted effort to downplay the significance of the events of 1649 and Krypiakevych's initial survey work did not continue. While new information related to the Treaty of Zboriv was published in the West, it was only in the early 1990s that Ukrainian and Polish scholars had the opportunity to turn their attention to the 1649 campaign.[7] Perhaps the most important contribution of the last decade was the publication of two engineering field military maps from the 1649 campaign (one from Zboriv and one from Zbarazh), which illustrates the disposition of forces and the extended fieldworks.[8]

In Ukraine, battlefield studies have a long tradition, but as elsewhere, it has focused almost exclusively on

Seventeenth century engravings of Cossack infantry and a mounted officer.

sites such as camps, castles and fortresses. The best-known exception to this was Shvechnikov's excavations at the 1651 Cossack Battle of Berestechko, where, over the course of multiple field seasons, he excavated numerous graves from a swamp bog.[9] The waters of the swamp prevented the looting of the dead and preserved significant amounts of organic materials. These particular environmental conditions preserved significant quantities of military arms and accoutrements as well as many personal items. By focusing on the swamps to the rear of the actual battlefield, Shvechnikov recovered items such as stocked muskets, arrows with preserved shafts, belts, and leather cartridge boxes. Since he found these artefacts with individual combatants, it is possible to reconstruct how these forces were armed and equipped.[10]

While the Berestechko excavations provide an unparalleled view of the peasants and Cossacks who died while fleeing after their defeat, Shvechnikov's excavations follow the traditional archaeological field

Cartridge box and its contents, recovered from the Berestechko Battlefield. Item on display at the Berestechko Battlefield Museum.

methods of digging in a very small area. Since battles occurred over a wide area, sometimes encompassing hundreds of square kilometres, an excavation method that relies on the analysis of a few square metres produces, in most instances, very few results. At Berestechko, researchers did not subject the rest of the battlefield to significant testing.[11] Even with the identification of individual artefacts, no research methodology existed at that time which could document the distribution of artefacts over many square kilometres. Not surprisingly, when in the mid-1990s, archaeologists employed traditional testing methods at the Cossack 1649 Zboriv battlefield, they failed to find any material from the seventeenth century battle.[12]

The study of open warfare, besides a few well-publicised successes such as Berestechko or Wisby,[13] began in earnest only after the work on the Little Bighorn battlefield was published.[14] The use of metal detectors at the Little Bighorn provided a way for archaeologists to deal with the limitations of identifying the distribution of battlefield artefacts over great distances. This data, coupled with extensive primary historical research and topographic information, allowed scholars to deal with the conditions specific in the study of battlefields. Using a similar approach, it was hoped to learn more

Equipment and weapons of a Polish Hussar from the mid-seventeenth century, Warsaw Military Museum.

about the Cossacks and their wars for freedom by studying the battlefields of these wars.

In 2001, the author, working with scholars in both Poland and Ukraine, initiated the Cossack Battlefield Commission to explore and study Cossack battlefields.[15] Beginning in 2002, the author, working in conjunction with the L'viv Institute of Ukrainian Studies and Bohdan Strotsen, the regional director in charge of preservation of historical and cultural monuments for the Ternopil oblast, began a joint survey, the purpose of which was to identify any possible remaining cultural resources associated with the military events of 1649. After integrating the primary accounts of the battle with the historical and geographic topography of the area, we conducted a visual inspection of the territory. Based on this preliminary analysis, areas that appear to have been least impacted by modern development were selected in Zboriv and Zbarazh.

The methodology employed was a variation on the one initially employed by Scott. As at the Little Bighorn

The terrain surrounding the town of Zboriv.

Volunteers and students working together in Zboriv.

battlefield, where both Native Americans and White Americans worked together to gain a better understanding of their shared past, both Polish and Ukrainian students laboured jointly in the fields of Zboriv and Zbarazh. Once a possible area was identified, students swept the fields using metal detectors. The types of metal detectors used locate small artefacts on the surface and reach an optimal depth of up to twenty centimetres. However, since the cone of the detector produced an egg shaped ellipse, the area scanned at the apex of the cone was very small - only the size of a coin. Along the ground surface the instrument surveyed an area directly proportional to the 8½" diameter of the detector's sensing coil. As water, rain, atmospheric pressure and a host of other factors affect the detectors, many scholars return to the same fields year after year and continue to retrieve artefacts.

Once a detector registered an object, the artefact was retrieved from the disturbed soil. Since the areas around Zboriv and Zbarazh have been subject to repetitive ploughing for generations, all the artefacts are lacking stratigraphic provenience and were treated as coming from the surface. Each recovered artefact was placed in a separate plastic bag and the find spot was marked with a wooden stake. For easier recognition, the stake had a red strip of cloth tied to it and the artefact in its bag was attached to this stake.

Following the students with the metal detectors was a person responsible for recording the co-ordinates of each artefact. Using a hand-held Global Positioning System (GPS) unit, we recorded the coordinates of each find and collected the artefacts from the field. Given the scale of the battlefield and number of square kilometres associated with it, an accuracy of +5m

Taking a GPS reading for a recovered artefact.

119

Another artefact comes to light.

provided by the GPS was considered to be acceptable. Following the cleaning of the finds, members of the project weighed, measured, drew and photographed each artefact. At the end of the field season, all the artefacts were presented to the local regional museum in Zboriv and Zbarazh.

A wide variety of artefacts, many of which date to the seventeenth century, were recovered during the course of the survey.[16] However, since these areas have been in agriculture for centuries, our initial analysis was restricted to distinctly seventeenth century military artefacts. Unlike medieval battlefields where very little datable military material exists, by the seventeenth century firearms were widely used, which allows scholars to recover quantities of lead balls and iron shot. As expected, we recovered quantities of musket balls and iron shot during our survey. When we plotted out the distribution of the seventeenth century military ordinance along an X and Y grid, at both sites we identified a line of dropped and impacted balls. Based on this preliminary information, we believe that we

'If we add to our datasets the existing contemporary maps of the 1649 campaign, we can clearly identify component parts of the battle.'

have discovered the eastern portion of a battle line at Zboriv in an area not yet subject to residential or industrial development. At Zbarazh, we have identified all three siege lines, but because of urban growth, only the most outward siege line has been preserved.

In both instances, when we take this distribution of military artefacts and compare them with the local topography, we see that all of these items are found along the military crest of small hills at both Zboriv and Zbarazh. Since the 'choice of ground on which to fight and the exact deployment of troops in battalia were based on sound military principles', it is clear that the topographic environment predetermined the establishment of the firing line in this particular location.[17] If we add to our datasets the existing contemporary maps of the 1649 campaign, we can clearly identify component parts of the battle.

In addition to the recovered ordnance, we also examined artefacts such as buttons, melted pieces of lead and quantities of hand wrought iron, which may relate to military wagons or weapons. Since it is unlikely that peasants could afford such items, there is a tendency to associate these items with the battle.

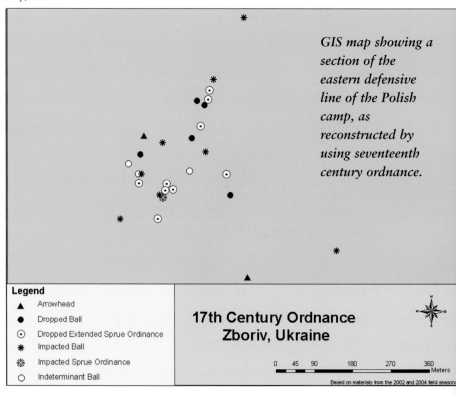

GIS map showing a section of the eastern defensive line of the Polish camp, as reconstructed by using seventeenth century ordnance.

Legend
- ▲ Arrowhead
- ● Dropped Ball
- ☉ Dropped Extended Sprue Ordinance
- ✳ Impacted Ball
- ✺ Impacted Sprue Ordinance
- ○ Indeterminant Ball

**17th Century Ordnance
Zboriv, Ukraine**

0 45 90   180   270   360
Meters

Based on materials from the 2002 and 2004 field seasons

As has previously been noted, unless it is possible to demonstrate a direct relationship between the military and non-military artefacts, no correlation may be postulated. However, since many of the objects were found along the same line as the dropped bullets, the likelihood of direct correlation between these artefacts is quite high.

According to a contemporary account of the battle, written shortly after the end of hostilities, the crown forces built earthen fortifications to strengthen their battle lines.[18] Although the eastern line of these earthen fortifications witnessed no major military engagements, the documentary record is quite clear that Tatar troops demonstrated in this area to draw the attention of the enemy.[19] The recovery of buttons and metal buckles among dropped musket balls, which we believe troops dropped when they prepared for battle, confirms the location of the eastern section of the Polish defensive earthworks at Zboriv.

The construction of the earthen walls on the night between the first and second day of the battle, while undertaken primarily by attached servants, required the assistance of combat troops. The dire situation in which the Crown army found itself, required haste and they would have used any item to build up a barricade. The Commonwealth commonly used heavy military wagons; similar to the fifteenth century *wagenburg* initially developed by Jan Ziska, the commander of the Hussite Armies of Bohemia, as mobile field defences. The recovery of so many metal hardware wagon parts found alongside seventeenth century military ordinance suggests that the army added wagons to the defensive barriers.

To recognise the implications of the distribution patterns of the recovered military ordnance, it is essential to understand how military units functioned and the role that firearms played in particular regiments as any gaps between groups of lead balls may indicate the space between musketeers occupied by pikemen, rather than two separate units. In the 1640s, musketeers generally represented only 2/3 of a European infantry regiment, as the remaining 1/3 were pikemen. Among infantry regiments, the general military practice of the period placed pike armed troops in the centre with musketeers on each flank. Within each army this arrangement may have been slightly different. The Swedish armies of King Gustavus Adolphus maintained a theoretical proportion of 216 pikes to 192 musketeers, while slightly larger Dutch battalions strived to maintain a ratio of 250 to 240.[20] In the 1630s, the Polish infantry was reorganised

'...an infantry battle line from the 1630s may have occupied a much smaller area of frontage than an infantry battle line of the 1660s.'

and followed both the Swedish and Dutch models which divided regiments into six companies. As the Polish army at Zboriv also included various 'German' mercenary troops, the relationship between pike and shot may have varied even between regiments.

Throughout the seventeenth century, there was a growing tendency to reduce the depth of infantry units. Rather than have units of ten or eight ranks deep, these were continuously reduced until reaching a rank of three or four deep by the early eighteenth century. During this evolution, regiments began increasingly to occupy a larger frontage but retained the same number of men. Thus, an infantry battle line from the 1630s may have occupied a much smaller area of frontage than an infantry battle line of the 1660s. Since most military units were rarely at full strength, the distribution of ordnance will not necessarily coincide with the theoretical dimensions of a combat unit.

Trying to link this material with particular Cossack regiments is even more difficult since the relationship between pike and shot within the regiments present at Zboriv remains unclear. Contemporary descriptions of the Cossack regiments suggest that many of the peasant troops were inadequately armed, with a third of the troops lacking firearms. However, since Khmelnytsky brought only his best troops to Zboriv while the rest of the Cossack army, including the newly raised peasant armies remained at Zbarazh, the majority of these troops were believed to have been armed with projectile weapons.

Our work at Zbarazh focused on the territory immediately surrounding the sixteenth century castle and its earthworks, as well as trying to establish the area of the 1649 siege. A comparison of the recently uncovered 1649 military engineering map with more modern topographic maps indicated that the most intensely defended area was to the northeast of the castle. An examination of the territory directly adjacent to the castle produced few surface finds from the seventeenth century, but we did encounter a large calibre ball lying directly on top of an earthen bank. This ball, which had a diameter of almost 40mm, was most likely from a small cannon, a *tarashnytsia*, but it remains unclear if it relates to the 1649 siege.

While housing has destroyed the area of the last two siege lines, that of the first line has remained in crop. Recently the area belonged to a collective farm, but now small parcels of land have been given to individual residents to use as gardens. Conducting our survey along

Iron arrowhead recovered from the Zboriv Battlefield.

ZBORIV REGIONAL MUSEUM.

An ancient engraving of a Tatar warrior holding a traditional style bow. The Cossacks employed such weapons due to the fact they were quicker to fire and were not affected by cold and wet weather conditions.

public footpaths and on those parcels which were not in crop, we encountered a significant amount of varied military ordnance. Lead balls were the most common item encountered, but iron arrowheads, axe heads, gun-flints, and sword fragments were also found.

By correlating the area where the most significant finds were encountered with the military map, we realised that the material was coming directly from a siege line. To test our hypothesis, Bohdan Strotsen excavated a test trench. This 1 x 4 metre trench exposed the remains of a ditch.[21] The lack of any datable materials from the ditch prevents us definitively linking this feature with the military events from the mid-seventeenth century, but the recovery of significant amounts of military ordnance from the immediate area clearly supports the idea that we had indeed encountered part of the initial siege line.

In the middle of the seventeenth century there was a great variation in the types of projectile weapons in use. In addition to firearms, Cossacks often made use of Tatar style bows, which, according to a seventeenth century French military engineer who had spent many years in the Commonwealth, had a faster rate of fire, could be used in adverse weather and did not give away the position of the bowman.[22] Although the recovery of seventeenth-century Tatar style arrowheads from the area of the siege of Zbarazh and at Berestechko confirms their continued use by the Cossacks, lead balls outnumber arrowheads on these battlefields at a ratio of 16 balls for every one arrowhead. Clearly, firearms

'...lead balls outnumber arrowheads on these battlefields at a ratio of 16 balls for every one arrowhead'.

were the primary weapons in use.

In Ukraine, modern flintlocks had, for the most part, replaced hazardous matchlocks by the middle of the seventeenth century. Excavations at the 1651 Berestechko battlefield indicated the overall dominance of flintlock weapons, while the recovery of large quantities of iron spanners suggests the use of expensive wheel locks. The lack of matchlock weapons, however, is surprising. Cheap and somewhat reliable, matchlocks were the dominant firearm during the English Civil War (1642-48)[23] and remained in use

Seventeenth century cannon balls recovered in the area around the modern town of Zboriv. ZBORIV REGIONAL MUSEUM.

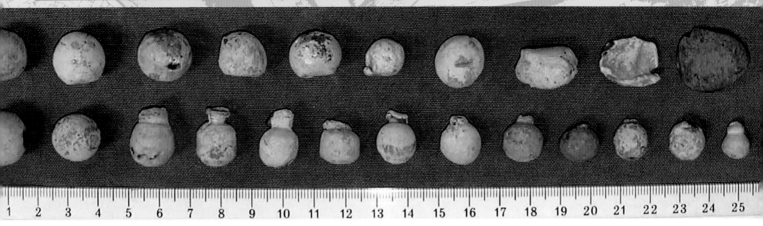

Examples of balls recovered from Zboriv during the 2002 and 2004 survey. ZBORIV REGIONAL MUSEUM.

The most dominant firearm of the time, the matchlock. Such weapons were used in the English Civil War and were cheap and easy to use.

by Austrian military units at least until the 1683 Siege of Vienna.[24] French and English armies retained matchlocks until the turn of the century. Yet among the 'poorly armed Cossacks', matchlocks were obsolete by the middle of the seventeenth century.

Another common assumption is the lack of firearm standardisation. Rebel armies often have logistical nightmares and given the significant variations in the firearm calibres, one would expect to find a wide range of musket ball calibres. Since all seventeenth century gunpowder left a residue of unburned soot after only a few shots, the barrel quickly became clogged and increasingly difficult to load. Conventional wisdom is that soldiers usually carried a variety of smaller balls to use as the battle progressed. Yet the recovery of complete bullet pouches and cartridge cases from Berestechko indicates no significant variations of ammunition calibres carried by each combatant. From this information we can make a much stronger argument that the calibre of ball corresponds closely to the weapons used.

A study of collections of seventeenth century military arms in both the National Army Museum in Warsaw (Poland) and the Historical Arsenal Museum in L'viv (Ukraine) clearly illustrates that seventeenth century armies standardised their weapon systems. Muskets, usually of Western European design, were

Close view of extended sprue ordnance. ZBORIV REGIONAL MUSEUM.

predominantly large calibre weapons with a bore diameter between 24 and 18 mm, with 20 mm being the most common. In 1649 and at the beginning of 1650 the arsenal in Warsaw acquired 1,300 muskets from Holland and 210 Dutch muskets.[25] Most oriental 'Turkish' weapons in the museums of Poland and Ukraine have a much smaller bore, while mid-seventeenth century Dutch muskets have a barrel bore that approaches 21 mm.[26] Given latitude for windage - that is, the difference between the actual barrel diameter and the size of the ball, the large calibre musket balls recovered from Zboriv may have come from the Dutch guns imported by the Polish Crown. The battlefield museum at Berestechko identified similar large size musket balls as 'bullets that killed Cossacks'.[27]

Most musket balls recovered from this area of the battlefield of Zboriv are between 11 and 16 mm. Given the close proximity of these finds along a line of battle, it is possible that these rounds all belonged to a particular military unit. In the seventeenth century, dragoons carried a specific type of firearm, called a *bandolet*. This weapon was of a smaller calibre and preserved examples in the museums of Poland and Ukraine have a bore diameter of between 18 and 11 mm, with diameters of 15 to 16 mm most common. At the same time, however, other cavalry units used smaller

123

calibre weapons. In addition, eastern firearms tended to be of a smaller calibre. While some have suggested that it may be possible in the future to identify certain types of units by the calibre of the shot, the use of small calibre weapons on both sides of the conflict precludes such an analysis. Nevertheless, the recovery of numerous large calibre balls may serve as an indicator for infantry in the service of the Polish crown.

During our survey we discovered a great variation in the actual musket balls. Unlike most projectiles that are round or exhibit uncut sprue from their casting, many of those recovered at Zboriv had an added or modified tail along the sprue, which is far more elaborate than a simple by-product of the casting process. Such additions are unusual, and besides being recovered at Berestechko and Zbarazh, have previously been rarely recognised as such in the archaeological record. A sprue is normally created as part of the casting process, but usually it is removed before the ball is fired. As such, unless a scholar is specifically looking for such sprues, they would most likely conclude that these were unfinished balls.

Yet these are not simply unfinished balls. As can be seen in the photograph on page 123, there exists a recess cavity on the top of the sprue. When compared with a regular ball that has not had its sprue trimmed off, one can clearly see that these sprue tails were intentionally created. Unlike eighteenth century cartridges, where both the ball and powder were inside a paper tube, makers of these earlier cartridges attached the paper tube to the sprue. Sometimes a special flange was added to the ball to help tie the paper cartridge. While such cartridges may have been in use by the mid-sixteenth century, in 1697, Saint Remy, a French scholar, 'illustrated a cartridge with a ball attached by its sprue as the latest type'.[28]

It is more than likely that the musket balls recovered at Zboriv were modified in such a manner to allow for the production of semi-fixed ammunition. An examination of the Cossack bullet moulds recovered at Berestechko indicates that at least some of them were modified to create extended sprues ordnance.

The production of cartridges simplified the loading process. Previously, musketeers relied upon bandoliers of pre-measured powder charges. Lord Orrery, a seventeenth century military writer noted that

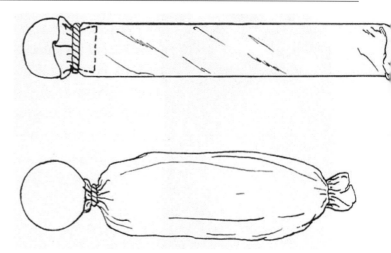

Seventeenth century paper cartridges with ball attached by the sprue. TAKEN FROM HAROLD L. PETERSON, ARMS AND ARMOR IN COLONIAL AMERICA.

'bandeleers are often apt to take fire, especially if the matchlock musket be used'.[29] The results of such accidents could be quite lethal. Although mounted units used small metal cartridge boxes as early as the second half of the sixteenth century, the overwhelming majority of European infantry continued to rely upon the dangerous bandoliers. The leather and wood cartridge boxes recovered at Berestechko are thought to be among the earliest known examples of infantry cartridge boxes used in Europe but it is more than likely that the Swedes first developed infantry cartridge boxes. Cartridge boxes quickly became popular and in 1656, for example, seventy-five cartridge boxes were included in an inventory list of munitions sent to the South River of New Netherlands.

A second advantage of the sprue, especially in small calibre bullets that are fired at a low muzzle velocity, is that the bullet tumbles - that is it does not fly symmetrically, but rather wobbles through the air. While such a weapon system may not have the range of a more powerful large calibre ball, the wounds inflicted in such a manner can be horrific. Such small calibre weapons, especially with tumbling munitions, use less gunpowder and are just as effective as large calibre weapons. The immediate benefit of such a system is that it allows troops to carry more rounds on the battlefield. The advantage of carrying more rounds over a reduced muzzle velocity had been recognized by military forces around the world for more than a century and the history of small arms development over the last hundred years reflects this tendency.

'Lord Orrery, a seventeenth century military writer noted that 'bandeleers are often apt to take fire, especially if the matchlock musket be used'. The results of such accidents could be quite lethal.'

The recovery of glass beads from an ammunition pouch at Berestchko also suggests that glass bullets, commonly used in the Commonwealth at the end of the sixteenth and at the beginning of the seventeenth century, may have also been used during the time of the Cossack wars. To date no such bullets have yet been recovered from either Zboriv or Zbarazh, but it is possible that such balls, like the one recovered from Putsk in northern Poland, were used.[30]

The recovered military ordnance challenges many of the commonly held assumptions of the Cossack armies of the mid-seventeenth century. Most scholars agree that the Cossack rebels wanted to create a new political system that would replace the religious, economic and cultural elite in the southeastern territories of the Commonwealth, but few also note that the military innovations employed by Cossacks were just as revolutionary. Not only were the rebel armies under the direction of innovative leaders who had significant military talent and expertise in engineering but also the weapons systems used by the rebels were the most modern and technically developed in both Europe and Asia. Clearly, these armies may have looked rather ragged, especially when compared to the silver and gold encrusted troops of the Commonwealth, but the Cossack army was a professional force equal to any on two continents.

Without doubt, the Cossack army was a professional fighting force. The image of a rag-tag mob, although burned in the collective memory, is a stereotype of limited value. Rather, while often clothed in non-regulated clothing and perhaps intermittently fed, these rebels, including long-serving Cossacks, former serfs, nobles and Orthodox clergy adopted and adapted new military tactics and weapon systems. This may not be all that unusual, since these same revolutionaries were, by their very nature, vying to bring about a new social reality. Although existing military establishments are often among the most conservative segments of society, the results of the research from this programme suggests that this rebel army, much like earlier and later revolutionary armies, adapted and incorporated the most recent and successful of the new technologies.

The identified sections of the battle lines serve as a point of reference for further research. By taking into consideration any minute topographic features in the terrain that contemporary military commanders would have exploited to their advantage, it is possible to correlate the terrain with the features noted on the preserved 1649 maps. Using this information, it becomes much easier to see how the actual battle developed. As the 1649 siege map of Zboriv also shows the disposition of particular units in the Crown's camp, with further

Flag allegedly carried at the Battle of Zboriv by Crown forces. WARSAW MILITARY MUSEUM.

work it may be possible to link the discovered ordnance with a particular military unit. Additional analysis will not only allow us to identify sections of the battlefield where cultural resources may be present, but also it will allow us to reconstruct the location of the earthworks even in areas significantly impacted by modern development.

When compared with other battlefield survey projects, our results at Zboriv were not unusual. For ten years Dan Sivilich and his group of excavators have been returning to the same areas of the American Revolutionary War battlefield of Monmouth (New Jersey) and continue to flesh out the original model. After a decade's worth of research, they are now able to show how and why the battle developed in the way it did. Clearly, the results achieved at Zboriv and Zbarazh reflect the possibilities offered in studying battlefields and need to be continued. By using new technologies, coupling them with local topography and comparing this information with the available documentary evidence, it is possible to gain further insights into one of the most studied and important events in the history of Ukraine and East Central Europe. Perhaps, and most importantly, it allows us to give a voice to a people who previously have not had the opportunity to speak for themselves.

Dr Adrian Mandzy is an Associate Professor at Morehead University, Kentucky USA.

NOTES

[1] Cossacks who chose to live in the Sich did so in stern simplicity without wives or families. The men were organized into military units and worked together for a common good.

[2] Although most people think of Cossacks as horse mounted troops, their earliest renown was as sailors who raided the Ottoman settlements along the Black Sea coast. During the middle of the seventeenth century, most Cossacks fought on foot or served as artillerymen.

[3] Originally from the German word *Hauptmann*. Among the Ukrainian Cossacks, the Hetman was the highest military, administrative and judicial office. This is not to be confused with the use of the title in the Commonwealth, where the term of hetman simply meant commander-in-chief and the highest military authority in the realm.

[4] Although the text of the Treaty of Zboriv has survived and the register of Cossacks has been previously published, Ukrainian scholars such as the eminent historian Mykhailo Hrushevsky has interpreted the Zboriv Agreement as 'hopeless' (Mykhailo Hrushevsky, *History of Ukraine-Rus'*, vol. 8, Canadian Institute of Ukrainian Studies Press, Toronto, 2002, pp 575-654) or 'compromised' (I. Krypiakevych, *Bohdan Khmelnyts'kyj*, Kiev, 1954, pp 165-172). More recently, the Canadian Ukrainian historian Frank Sysyn has indicated that 'the guarantee of a forty-thousand-man Cossack army ensured Hetman Khmel'nyts'kyj his place as an almost independent ruler of the Ukraine' (Frank Sysyn, *Between Poland and Ukraine: The Dilemma of Adam Kysil 1600-1653*, Cambridge, MA, 1985, p. 173).

[5] While many scholars have devoted their attention to the battle of Zboriv, among the earliest and most influential studies remain L. Kubala, *Oblężenie Zbaraża i pokój pod Zborowem, Szkice historyczne*, Krakow, 1896 and Ludwik Frąs, *Bitwa pod Zborowem w r. 1649*, *Kwartalnik Historzcynz*, XLVI, 1932.

Above: Monument to the Battle of Zboriv that was put up on site in the 1990s.

Burial mound traditionally attributed to the Battle of Zboriv. Surface testing in the area around the mound uncovered seventeenth century balls and large quantities of twentieth century ordnance.

[6] I. Krypiakevych published five separate accounts of the battle of Zboriv, but the most detailed description appears in *Zhyttia i Znannia*, no. 10-11, L'viv, 1929. A later account published by the same author in the *Litopys Chervonoi Kalyny*, no. 10, L'viv, 1931, includes two maps, one which showed the disposition of forces at the time of the initial ambush, and second illustrated the attacks of the second day. These two maps were later reprinted (Ivan Tyktor, *Istoriia Ukrains'koho Vijs'ka*, Winnipeg, 1953).

[7] Teodir Matskiv, 'Zborivs'kyj Dohovir u svitli nimets'koi j anhlijs'koi presy z 1649 r', *Zborivshchyna*, Naukove Tovarystvo im Shevchenka, Ukrains'kyj Arkhiv, vol. 38, Toronto, 1985.

[8] Stanislaw Alexandrowicz, 'Plany Obronnych Obozów wojsk Polskich pod Zbara´zem i Zborowem z Roku 1649', *Fortyfikacja*, vol. 1, 1995, pp 15-23.

[9] I. K. Sveshnikov, *Bytva pid Berestechkom*, L'viv, 1993.

[10] Aleksej Vasyl'ev and Igor Dzys, 'Bytva pod Berestechkom', *Zeughaus*, Moscow, No. 8, (2/1988), pp 2-6.

[11] Such a result is not unexpected, since archaeologists who have relied on traditional testing methods of digging in depth rarely have been successful in identifying resources related to military engagements. Using traditional archaeological field methods at the American Civil War First Manassas (Bull Run) battlefield, for example, 'only one artefact was found by shovel testing, while several hundred were found using metal detectors' (Lawrence E. Babits, 'Book Archaeology of the Cowpens battlefield', *Fields of Conflict: Progress and Prospect in Battlefield Archaeology*, P.W.M. Freeman and A. Pollard, eds., BAR International Series 958, 2001, p. 118).

[12] Artefacts from these excavations are on display at the local museum in Zboriv.

[13] Excavations of a burial pit from the Battle of Wisby, for example, provided a good indication of medieval warfare (Bengt Thordeman, Poul Noörlund and Bo E. Ingelmark, *Armour from the Battle of Wisby, 1361*, vol. 1, Kungl. Vitterhets Historie OCH Antikvitets Akademien, Stockholm, 1939).

[14] Douglas D. Scott and Richard A. Fox, Jr., *Archaeological insights into the Custer battle: an assessment of the 1984 field season*, Norman, 1987; and D. D. Scott, R. A. Fox, Jr., M. A. Connor and D. Harmon, *Archaeological perspectives on the Battle of the Little Bighorn*, Norman, 1989.

[15] For more information about the Commission and to view the results of the first year's programme, please go to the following web site: **www.lviv.ua/cossacks**

[16] At Zboriv, and to a lesser degree at Zbarazh, the most common artefacts recovered from the survey data are from later battles in this area. Shrapnel balls, rifle cartridges, bullets and artillery shell fragments from the First World War and the Polish-Ukrainian War of 1919 litter the areas of both 1649 battlefields, while other military equipment, such as the early nineteenth century Russian button found at Zbarazh, which may relate to the military events of 1809, were also periodically encountered.

[17] Glenn Foard, 'The archaeology of attack: battles and sieges of the English Civil War', in *Fields of Conflict: Progress and Prospect in Battlefield Archaeology*, P.W.M. Freeman and A. Pollard, eds., BAR International Series 958, 2001, p. 89.

[18] Valerij Smolij and Valerij Stepankov, *Bohdan Khmelnytskyj*, Kiev, 2003, p. 200.

[19] Ivan Krypiakevych, 'Z Istorii Zborova', p. 25.

[20] Thomas E. Griess, senior editor, *The Dawn of Modern Warfare*, The West Point Military History Series, Wayne, 1984, p. 48.

[21] B. S. Strotsen', *Zvit pro arkheolohichni rozvidky v okolytsiakh m. Zbarazha (Ternopil's'ka obl.) u 2003 r.*, Ternopil, 2004.

[22] Guillaume Le Vasseur, le Sieur de Beauplan, *Description D'Ukranie* [1660], L'viv, 1998.

[23] Tony Pollard and Neil Oliver, *Two Men in a Trench: Battlefield Archaeology - The Key to Unlocking the Past*, London, 2002, p. 211.

[24] Das Heeresgeschichtliche Museum (Museum of Military History), Vienna, Austria.

[25] Konstanty Górski, *Historya Artyleryi Polskiej*, Warszawa, 1902, p. 121.

[26] For a discussion of exported arms from Holland, see Jan Piet Puype, 'Dutch and Other Flintlocks from Seventeenth Century Iroquois Sites', in *Proceedings of the 1984 Trade Gun Conference*, Research Records, No.18, Vol. 1, Rochester Museum and Science Center, Rochester, 1985.

[27] Museum of the 'Cossack Mounds', National Historical Memorial Preserve 'Field of the Berestechko Battle', Pliasheva Village, Radyvylivs'kyj Region, Rivnens'ka oblast, Ukraine.

[28] Pierre Surirey de Saint Remy, *Memoires d'Artillerie*, second edition, 2 vol, Paris, 1707.

[29] Harold L. Peterson, *Arms and Armor in Colonial America 1526-1783*, Harrisburg, Pennsylvania, 1956, p. 63.

[30] Courtesy of Professor Jerzy Kruppè, University of Warsaw, Poland.

REVIEWS

Beneath Flanders Fields
The Tunnellers' War 1914-18

PETER BARTON, PETER DOYLE AND JOHAN VANDEWALLE

SPELLMOUNT BOOKS

ISBN: 1-86227-237-9

Hardback £25.00

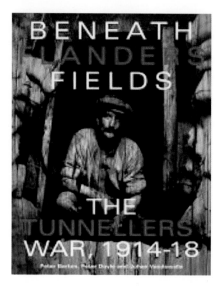

I SHOULD, I SUPPOSE, DECLARE AN INTEREST in this book at the outset. That interest stems neither from the fact that I have played any part in its writing or production, which I have not - nor is it because I have in the past worked with at least two of its authors - which I have - it runs, no pun intended for a book about tunnelling, much deeper than that, into the very subject matter with which the authors deal.

Born, bred and educated in South Yorkshire during the 1960s and 70s one could not escape a connection with the coal mining industry. My father, both my grandfathers and their fathers before them had all worked at one 'pit' or another in several of the many mines then in production in and around the Barnsley area. My maternal grandfather had both his legs broken - twice - in rock falls underground and one of his brothers was killed in a mining accident. My wife, also from South Yorkshire, never saw her paternal grandfather. He was killed along with 57 other men in a terrific explosion which incinerated the coalface at a colliery called Wharncliffe Woodmoor as late as 1936. Illness, injury and even death were part of the fabric of life in such communities. Stories of a working life spent in hazardous conditions hundreds of feet below ground; of the trials and tribulations, of the suffering and sacrifice and yes, even the humour and comradeship, were commonplace in my family and scores of others just like it.

But there have been miners, of one sort or another, with us for hundreds of years and there can be little doubt that they are a race apart. It took - it takes still - a certain kind of person to be a miner. It is not natural for human beings to turn away from the light, the open spaces and life giving oxygen and instead to burrow deep into the earth whilst at the same time accepting the inherent risks of taking on powerful forces of nature, of complex geology and the laws of physics and chemistry. Mining is a dangerous enough occupation in peacetime, witness the many monuments erected to those killed in mining accidents around the UK, but set it in the context of the first war of the industrial age and throw high explosives and a tenacious, professional and committed enemy into the mix, then the task of mine warfare becomes almost impossible to imagine.

That we can even begin to imagine the problems faced by the military tunnellers of WW1, toiling away in their dank, secret and claustrophobic war against the German *pionere* and begin to grasp the tantalising possibilities which advances in science and technology offered the sappers in order to surmount them, is a testament to the care and devotion to the subject matter, to the people involved and to the depth of research evident on every page of this book.

By combining their considerable personal experience, interests and professional expertise the authors have assembled a triumvirate in which the reader can trust absolutely. Even the most cursory of glances at the preface and the list of names of those who have assisted the authors during their quarter century of research - acknowledged experts in military topography and mapping, cutting edge battlefield archaeology, unexploded ordnance recovery and ongoing exploration and analysis of WW1 subterranean systems - only serves to reinforce that sense of trust.

There have been few books on the tunnellers' war. It is almost 70 years since the publication of Grant Grieve and Newman's *Tunnellers* and over 40 since Alexander

Barrie's seminal *War Underground*. The former - published in honour of the tunnellers' efforts - contained much technical detail about mining and is not an accessible read whilst the latter, relying heavily on the many personal accounts gathered by the author, is 'image light'. Anyone reading the descriptions in Barrie's book who has ever been down a mine or been potholing or caving and turned their helmet lamp off will be able to empathise with the conditions in which the tunnellers lived and worked but, as the authors rightly point out, for anyone else that empathy may be difficult to conjure. Hence the wish by the authors, during the long gestation of the project, to marry the myriad and often technical aspects of the disciplines on which military tunnelling draws, with numerous photographs, diagrams, maps and evocative first hand accounts from the tunnellers involved.

It is to their credit that the authors had the foresight to opt for a large format book printed on quality paper and with images in both black and white and colour in the pursuit of clarity. Indeed it is the very clarity of the images and their positioning with respect to, and allied with the clarity of the narrative, which is the major strength of this work.

From Peter Doyle's pithy and eminently readable opening paragraphs on what he terms the 'simple' geology of Flanders - although 'simple' might not have been the term that tripped off the lips of the 'moles' themselves, battling the ever present 'moisture' of the 'wet Flanders plain', Beneath Flanders Fields takes the reader on a remarkable and eye opening journey into every nook and cranny of the working lives, and often, lonely deaths, of the sappers of the Tunnelling Companies, Royal Engineers (RE). Although an oft-used device, the use of a 'quotable quote' as a scene setter for each chapter is no less effective for that as it readies the reader for what is to follow. And what follows is the history of military mining, the development of the RE Tunnelling Companies and mine warfare, rising steadily to a crescendo and the zenith of the tunnellers' art as witnessed on the opening day of the Battle of Messines in 1917, before turning, finally, to the tunnellers' role in the construction of the vast subterranean 'cities in the Ypres Salient' after the end of offensive mining operations in 1917. There is also an important section on the legacy of mining operations for the people now trying to earn a living on the 'wet Flanders plain' today as well as the implications for archaeological research in the area. In some areas of Flanders the famous clay has

> '...a sawn off .303 Lee Enfield rifle was the weapon of choice for close-quarters, 'breakthrough' fighting for some of the tunnellers'.

preserved entire systems 'complete in every detail', which are already helping to flesh out what the authors call the 'social history' of the war beneath the surface. There is more, much more, still to be discovered.

The writing is tight, always informative, and often humorous but never patronising and there is much original research here. I have, for example, already logged in my memory banks that a sawn off .303 Lee Enfield rifle was the weapon of choice for close-quarters, 'breakthrough' fighting for some of the tunnellers in the Bluff workings, a fact which will no doubt surface at some appropriate point in the future. I will, of course, cite the source when I use it! There are also abundant references and notes to stimulate months of further study for those who wish.

Woven throughout, however, are the personal accounts and testimonies of the 'moles' who fought this deep, dark and hidden war and these, perhaps, are really the heart and soul of the work. After all these are the words of the men who actually waged a war beneath a war. These were the men who sometimes became locked in a death struggle in the pitch darkness, in the confines of a 4'x3' tunnel by first feeling for the epaulettes on the other man's shoulders to ascertain whether he was, indeed, friend or foe. One can only gasp in awe at the sheer horror of combat in such a situation.

As this book is about tunnelling in Flanders, one can only hope that we do not have to wait another twenty-five years before the authors publish another volume on the mining operations in Artois and Picardy. As the descendant of generations of Yorkshire coal miners I shall certainly look forward to it. Apparently it was the skills and experience of the ex-colliers, which made them more suited for working in the harder chalk areas.

And speaking of Yorkshire colliers, I come to my one very small criticism and it surrounds a very brave Yorkshire coal miner indeed. On the back cover of the dust jacket Sapper William Hackett, the only tunneller VC of WW1, killed in action on 22 June 1916 and whose own 14 year old son had to have his leg amputated after a mining accident the month before, is pictured above a caption that claims he came from 'Mexborough, Nottinghamshire'. When I was at school Mexborough, and the selfless Sapper Hackett's previous place of employment - Manvers Main pit - was always in God's Own County. Perhaps that should have been checked by a Yorkshireman or woman.

Jon Cooksey

The Great Warbow
From Hastings to the Mary Rose

MATTHEW STRICKLAND & ROBERT HARDY

SUTTON PUBLISHING

ISBN: 0-7509-3167-1

Hardback £25.00

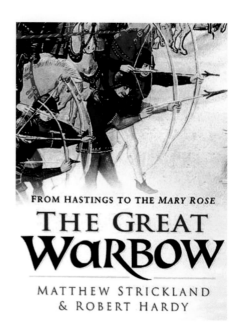

FROM HASTINGS TO THE MARY ROSE

THE GREAT WARBOW

MATTHEW STRICKLAND
& ROBERT HARDY

THIS VOLUME NEEDS ALL OF ITS WELL-PRODUCED and well illustrated 538 pages to cover the wide geographical and chronological range of its subject. From before Hastings through to the twilight of the warbow in Tudor England, and from the European Crusading armies in the Near East to Bruce's massive Scottish victory at Bannockburn in the Scottish War of Independence, this is an impressive tour de force that goes well beyond a simple exploration of the longbow itself. Given the critical role of the weapon in all aspects of warfare of the medieval period this is a welcome approach, but it provides the authors with a daunting challenge. The challenge is met with remarkable skill and thoroughness in what is an exceptionally well-referenced work, with 100 of the pages devoted to endnotes and bibliography, making it an important tool for every student of warfare of the medieval period.

The origins of the book lie in Robert Hardy's involvement in the conservation and testing of the 138 longbows and 2000 arrows recovered from the wreck of the Tudor warship, the *Mary Rose*. Though coming from the very last phase of the longbow's military significance, these artefacts have given us a unique perspective on warfare of the medieval period, for the capabilities of a weapon are a major determinant of its potential in battle. Hardy provides us with an engaging narrative on this *Mary Rose* research, which has demonstrated the awesome power of the warbow, revealing capabilities that many sceptical experts have finally had to accept. Later in the volume he also presents a valuable contribution on the tactical deployment of the bow in battle. But the greater part of the volume, as the unusual attributions at the end of each chapter or section reveal, is the work of Strickland. The two authors bring very different and complementary experience to the study: Hardy writing first and foremost from the perspective of an experienced archer who has worked with both original and modern 'approximation' bows and arrows of the Tudor period, while Strickland approaches the subject with an impressive grasp of the documentary record.

The longbow has for centuries held a special place in English history, both popular and academic, as the battle-winning weapon of the Hundred Years War and with a similar iconic status for us as the Spitfire in World War II. As the authors show, it was not a uniquely English weapon but it was one upon which English armies concentrated more than any other. At the height of its ascendancy in the 14th and 15th centuries, through its effective tactical deployment in vast numbers it won dramatic victories in battles such as Agincourt and Crecy, making English armies feared across Europe. Yet as Strickland demonstrates, it was not just in the 14th and 15th centuries that the longbow was a dominant force in open battle. This weapon had a much longer history, proving decisive in much earlier conflicts, as the accounts of the Battle of The Standard (Northallerton, 1138) provide us with the clearest confirmation.

This book traces the role and influence of the longbow in military action in Britain and Europe throughout the medieval period, and compares its character, use and effectiveness with its competing shot weapons: the composite bow, and particularly the crossbow and, latterly, hand held firearms. In so doing it provides new insight into the nature of battle as well as into the weapon itself. Hopefully it finally dispels that most damaging of myths for the understanding of medieval military conflict, that the longbow of Crecy was a new development in the later Middle Ages from a less effective short bow. With a balance of archaeological, written and graphic evidence, Strickland demonstrates the longbow's origins in prehistory and a continuity of use in warfare through the Anglo-Saxon period, as in descriptions in the poem *Beowulf* and its deployment at Maldon (Essex, 991), right through the medieval period, even in peripheral areas of Europe being employed in battle as late as the mid 17th century.

There are many themes to follow, but at the heart of the book lies a simple question that is, in reality, very hard to answer. Having demonstrated that the longbow's battle winning capabilities in the Hundred Years War did not represent a simple technological advance, as Oman had believed, Strickland seeks an alternative explanation. He explores the broad range of evidence and argument now available to us, balancing competing ideas. This follows many strands, such as the

'Hardy provides us with an engaging narrative on this *Mary Rose* research, which has demonstrated the awesome power of the warbow, revealing capabilities that many sceptical experts have finally had to accept.'

exploration of the dramatic shifts in tactics between the use of cavalry, fighting largely on foot supported by the bow, through a phase dominated by the heavy cavalry charge, shifting back again at least in English armies to dismounted cavalry in armies dominated by the longbow, following the dramatic reversal at Bannockburn in 1314. Even if, by the end, one does not feel that the question has been fully answered this is not the fault of the authors. Instead it reflects shortcomings of present knowledge and thus they provide us with pointers to important avenues for future research.

To a large degree the limitations of the book result from the decision to take on the full scope of the challenge, by including the study of the bow in battle. In doing so Strickland provides a welcome approach that rejects the extreme revisionist perspective that has for too long held sway, and is still vociferously presented in works such as Jones's

Bosworth. In reaction to what they see as a myopic, battle centred perspective on warfare displayed by military historians in the late 19th to mid 20th century, such as Oman and Burne, the study of the fine detail of battle has been abandoned by many historians. It has been dismissed as peripheral - simply the outmoded preserve of retired military men. This represents a mistaken rejection of a resource of great potential. Thankfully Strickland is unwilling to discard such potential. In scope, though most certainly not in detail, this new book harks back to the approach of Oman and Delbruck, of which the revisionists are so critical. In so doing it reasserts the importance of integrating battles into the analysis of warfare.

It is when handling the documentary evidence for the weapon itself, for the composition of armies, logistics and generalised discussion of strategy and tactics that the book is most convincing. Strickland has an impressive command of the primary and secondary sources and weaves the evidence together in a valuable overview of warfare of the period, though of course seen primarily from the perspective of one key weapon. The success of these aspects of the book is a tribute both to the scholarship of the authors and to the enormous advances in understanding that have been achieved by many others over past decades in these areas of research. It is when attempting to integrate this with the practical employment of the weapon in action that the problems begin.

At the outset Strickland admits the great difficulties posed by the study of battles, because 'the location of battles .... and hence the effect of topography upon them, is rarely known with any precision', difficulties compounded by the uncertainties in determining troop numbers and the problems posed by the fragmentary accounts of the action. But he recognises that these problems have to be faced, for 'one cannot study a weapon without at least attempting to discover how it performed in the role for which it was principally intended'. It was essential to examine the ways in which in different battles the tactics changed in response to terrain, troop numbers, military abilities and training and much more. Yet when reading the discussions of battles such as Bannockburn or Bosworth one realises how in such relatively brief discussion the uncertainties of current knowledge have to be skated over. Unfortunately the uncertainties are so great that one cannot at present draw the sort of conclusions about the

actions that Strickland seeks, for in both these battles, and indeed many more even where the actual site is not under such fundamental dispute, our knowledge of the reality of the historic terrain is wholly inadequate. Yet if one does not understand the terrain and the way in which the commanders exploited the opportunities it provided then there are severe limitations on the lessons one can draw from those battles. This should not, however, be taken as a criticism of the authors of this book. Rather it ought to be treated as a challenge to us, as students of battlefields, to develop our analysis of these sites to match the research that Strickland and Hardy and indeed many others have successfully pursued on the longbow and many other aspects of warfare of the medieval period. One can only hope that in work such as that underway at Towton, planned for Bosworth and being considered for Bannockburn, the interdisciplinary study of battlefields, including a major new contribution from archaeology, may eventually deliver the evidence and answers that are so clearly needed.

But one must not conclude a review of this important book on a critical note, however positive may be the challenges that flow from it, for this is an impressive volume that is a pleasure to read as well as a great work of scholarship. It will be enjoyed and employed by both the serious researcher and the more casual reader, for Strickland and Hardy have delivered a book that will long dominate its field, just as surely as did the weapon of which they write.

Glenn Foard

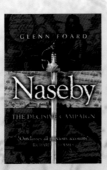

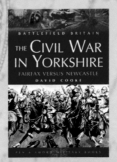

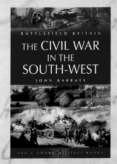

BROTHERS IN ARMS

ROAD TO HILL 30

BASED ON A TRUE STORY, BROTHERS IN ARMS tells the story of the men of the 101st Airborne paratroopers. Playing as squadron leader, Sgt. Matt Baker, the player must lead his men from their initial parachute drop on D-Day through to D+8.

What makes Brothers in Arms unique is the way in which the game ensures the player cares for the men in their squad. The game includes more than twenty characters, each having a distinctive and unique personality. Brothers in Arms ensures that more than being just other characters, these are men you develop a real attachment for. As the story unfolds, the player must choose between the lives of his men and the success of the mission.

The game is played as a first-person-shooter but has a strategic edge. Rather than simply blazing their way through the German Army, the player must use a number of tactics including fire and manoeuvre to outflank the enemy. To enable the player to do this the game contains a facility to pause the action and take an aerial 3D view of the battlefield to spot enemy positions and plan attacks.

Brothers in Arms is the most authentic

WW2 game created. An enormous amount of effort has been put into the game, ensuring that everything is as accurate as possible. Weapons featured in the game are exactly the same as those used by men of the 101st including M1 Garand, Tommy Gun, Mauser K98 and Colt M1911. The design of the levels ensures that featured towns appear as they would have in 1944. Every house, wall, hedgerow and field is positioned exactly as it would have been in the Second World War.

Graphically, Brothers in Arms is stunning. The game manages to combine accurate physics with fantastic level design. Soldiers are modelled authentically and move with amazing realism, ducking for cover, returning enemy fire and stopping to check on fallen comrades.

Brothers in Arms introduces the player slowly to the action and the earlier missions act as training levels. This ensures the game never becomes too complicated and once begun, the missions hook the player into wanting to carry on to see what will happen next.

Overall Brothers in Arms is a stunning game and comes highly recommended.

Brothers in Arms is out now for Xbox, Playstation 2 and PC.

MEDAL OF HONOR
EUROPEAN ASSAULT

THIS IS THE LATEST GAME IN THE MEDAL OF HONOR series and sees the player taking the role of William Holt, a US Army Lieutenant.

The main task in the game is to gather intelligence regarding the development and deployment of the Nazi Tiger Tank and preventing the Nazi plan to deploy atomic technology. To carry out this pursuit the player is thrust into action in all the major battles of World War Two in Europe.

Unlike Brothers in Arms, the Medal of Honor series is not overly realistic and is similar to a standard first-person-shooter. At times it really is like one man against the entire German Army.

Graphically the game is quite strong and the differing levels are well designed and fun to play through. However, the game is quite short and offers little in the way of replay value, so serious players may be slightly disappointed by how quickly the game is over. Anyone who enjoyed the earlier Medal of Honor games will like European Assault as it really is more of the same.

Medal of Honor: European Assault is out now for Xbox, Playstation 2 and Gamecube.

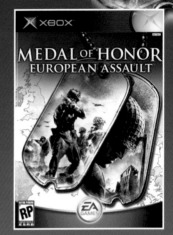

CALL OF DUTY
FINEST HOUR

This acclaimed PC game has now made its way onto the consoles. Call of Duty offers players the chance to experience the intensity and chaos of battles as their squadron fights its way through some of the key battles of World War Two. Featuring an immersive storyline, the player fights as soldiers from a number of allied countries as they battle the Nazi regime.

Although the game is very cinematic, the computer A.I. is a little unpredictable which can detract from the overall realism. Graphically the game is acceptable but is not in the same league as Brothers in Arms, although the sound is excellent.

This game really impressed on PC when it was released but has been slightly dumbed down for the consoles. Unfortunately this means the game is not as impressive as it could have been. Although still good fun, those wanting a little more detail would be better off with Brothers in Arms.

Call of Duty is out now for Xbox, Playstation 2, Gamecube and PC.